A Time to Be Deborah

A Time to Die

A Time to Be Deborah

JOYCE CARLIN

RESOURCE *Publications* • Eugene, Oregon

A TIME TO BE DEBORAH

Copyright © 2009 Joyce Carlin. All rights reserved. Except for brief quotations in critical publications or reviews, no part of this book may be reproduced in any manner without prior written permission from the publisher. Write: Permissions, Wipf and Stock Publishers, 199 W. 8th Ave., Suite 3, Eugene, OR 97401.

Resource Publications
A Division of Wipf and Stock Publishers
199 W. 8th Ave., Suite 3
Eugene, OR 97401

www.wipfandstock.com

ISBN 13: 978-1-60608-288-1

Manufactured in the U.S.A.

All scripture taken from the HOLY BIBLE, NEW KING JAMES VERSION, Copyright 1982 by Thomas Nelson, Inc.

*To my students
who continue to amaze and inspire me with their thoughtful
and often simple solutions to the issues of the day.
Our future is in good hands.*

Contents

Introduction ix

1 On Account of Deborah 1

2 Will the Real Judge Stand Up? 9

3 Are We There Yet? 26

4 Please Don't Repeat 34

5 Cycling for the Sake of the Kids 46

6 Sin Squared 53

7 The Enemy Is Us 60

8 Hope Revisited 72

9 Political CPR 81

10 Never Again, and This Time I Mean It! 91

11 That the Nation May Endure 97

12 The Sum of the Parts 104

Epilogue: Some Assembly Required 118

Salvation Invitation 123

Introduction

A Time to Be Deborah

THIS IS A BOOK about politics. It is political in the *truest* sense because it speaks to the duty of people to interact with integrity. It is not intended to be partisan or inflammatory. Indeed, I place this work before you to create and stimulate dialogue and to underscore the responsibility of Christian women to become politically active and prevent the election of government officials who stand for anti-God, anti-life, and anti-Christian ethics. That I may develop some piquant and seditious concepts is a foregone conclusion. Talk in this venue always causes heated discussion and often stirs up emotions. There is nothing wrong with vigorous debate. Our founding fathers accomplished much while vociferously questioning each other's common sense. Indeed, this opus has already generated some criticism from my husband who believes that the work is too intellectual. It is his belief that, in order to reach the maximum audience with my message, I must dumb it down a bit. The only problem with that recommendation is that it speaks to the very issue before me. We have become an impotent force in the world today *because* we are not engaging in intellectual dialogue and upper-level problem solving. If we truly hope to effect the outcome of political decisions in America today, we must become educated in the issues and able to "talk the talk" with the best of them. If this book is too intellectual for you, get a dictionary or a thesaurus and plug through it. It is no longer adequate to blame your poor education or simple vocabulary for the lack of action. As women in the church today, it is our solemn charge to protect our children from all that is evil. We *ourselves* must fight or get behind a champion and force the issues. It is feminine. It is worthy. It is courageous, and it is critical.

I am grateful that these are not my personal views alone since I am only the messenger and, therefore, must be covered by the disclaimer that prevents me from being shot. And so, in the midst of America's rush to become a society of tolerance and inclusion, the time has come to speak out and step out. Consequently, here I go, stomping and screaming into that good night, and hoping to send out a call to arms to Christian sisters everywhere that might save our country from certain destruction. I am not being reactionary. I am measuring the facts against God's Word. I am in good company, and we are not alone. There is a growing number of godly women marching in support of a return to morality and sanity in America.

Those on the other side are more vocal and fearless about broadcasting their message because they believe they speak for the era of the tolerant, an ignoble bunch at best. These confused minorities disdain who we are and what we believe and fight to muzzle us. Unfortunately, our team has more than one problem. I hope to educate and remediate, and, therefore, circumvent or prevent a disastrous outcome.

That this book will infuriate some is inevitable. But, my heroine did not care who she infuriated because she fought the good fight. I hope the same will be said about this work, even if only by what my opponents would label the "right-wing fanatics." Together, we shall all examine what I believe to be the greatest account of a woman of valor ever told. I speak of Deborah, judge and prophetess of Biblical fame. She was everything the women's movement proclaims to respect, and yet, she stood on the diametrically *opposite* side of every issue of current popularity. This is going to be fun!

1

On Account of Deborah

"Therefore know that the Lord your God, He is God, the faithful God who keeps covenant and mercy for a thousand generations with those who love Him and keep His commandments; and He repays those who hate Him to their face, to destroy them. He will not be slack with him who hates Him; He will repay him to his face."

Deuteronomy 7:9–10

I am hoping that you enjoy double entendre as much as I do. Otherwise, the title of this chapter will be lost to many. For purposes of clarification, I am convicted to use the word account and not the watered down and questionable term story. Many scholars, more educated than I, have verified the factual and historical basis for the Biblical details, definitively. It would be ridiculous for me to add my yea and amen to their intellectual conclusions. But, just so you know, I believe the Bible to be inerrant, God-breathed, and sufficient to answer all of life's questions.

In further reference to the title of the chapter however, I have set out on this journey because of a fascination and kindred connection to my illustrative character, the Prophetess Deborah. As an archetype for strong women, she is a no-fail example. Therefore, I have taken a factual, historical *account* that inspires and strengthens me to accept my own *accountability* for change in America and to suggest resolve from Christian women to enter what I believe to be the fight of our lives.

I have, probably, now lost the lunatic fringe, which is best because my opinions do not become more gentile. At any rate, those who have passed this work off as trash this early on need to be off forming their aluminum foil hats and listening for illuminati white noise in their backyards. I don't mean to be rude, but a true pundit of any philosophy knows that understanding your enemy is a key component to a successful offensive. If you want to know how conservative women think, stick around. (I recognize your need to make the obvious joke about having some brain matter removed before embarking on this task. Ha. Ha.) Let's just get on with the discussion and agree to disagree, initially, about the reference point.

THE BIBLE AS A HISTORICAL RESOURCE

The fascinating account of Deborah's life and ministry unfolds in the Biblical book of Judges. Now, in light of the current fuss over judges in our nation, this should be of some interest to us all. Remember, I proposed that *all* of life's important issues could be resolved by using Biblical advice. It would follow that good Christian folks would go there first and do as they are told. That is not the case, as can be observed by visiting the offices and libraries of learned professional people and noticing volume after volume of research materials and journals, intended to guide and educate them in their chosen field. So as not to waste the paper and bindings, some of our political leaders *do* use these epistles to filibuster instead of communicate, and so, the investment is not a total loss.

Nonetheless, it is quite acceptable in most learned circles to eliminate the Bible as a resource in the research process. In an environment of tolerance and liberal thought, this old, dusty Book is not respected as a quotable text and will often not be found among the prestigious volumes of the libraries of the high-minded. That is unfortunate, and it is also the first place that intellectuals go wrong. Many of today's high thinkers pass the Good Book off as fodder for the weak minded, most usually without the slightest scholarship backing the charge. This may be excusable if you are, say, a retired pro wrestler, but it smacks of laziness and fear-based rationalization from educated folk. I say if you are going to speak to a subject, inform yourself first-hand of the nature of the eliminated body of work.

When I began studying creation versus evolution, I read Darwin's work. How could I possibly determine the relevance of the theory if I did not educate myself in its content? That's the problem with my opponents in the political field. They don't do their homework. I'm a teacher, and I tell my students that is how we fail. And so, though there is a never-ending fountain of information to be enjoyed in our paper and cyber-space world, it is puzzling when an otherwise open-minded person rejects possible material.

On Account of Deborah 3

Please do keep the journals and leather-bound volumes. Just entertain the possible usefulness of knowing your enemy.

Disagree with me if you like, as we explore the wealth of information contained in the account of Barak and Deborah and the Israelite people in the Book of Judges. I am presenting this opinion mostly to the women of the church in preparation for what may be the most important presidential election in our history. The outcome of the 2008 election could be our opportunity to change the face of America from a liberal wasteland to the homeland intended by our founding fathers.

In order to facilitate our agreement on a reference point, it is important that the account in the fourth and fifth chapters of Judges be understood. The prophetess, Deborah, performed her duties within an approximate four hundred year cycle of judge/deliverers. With each experience of Israelite captivity, the subsequent oppression and its companion sinful behaviors loomed greater and darker. And so, Deborah's career was conducted in the midst of generational error.

As chapter four of Judges begins, we are informed that the people have again disobeyed the laws of God and are involved up to their foolish necks in sinful and degenerate practices. The preceding judge, Ehud, had died and left them hopefully honor-bound to glorify God. They did not. The cycle of sin and debauchery began again in earnest.

Deborah has been seated as the judge of the Israelites and their civil disputes and concerns. Daily, she hears complaints and makes rulings according to the Biblical laws. Her rulings are legally binding on her people. Deborah also hears from God on matters concerning the spiritual and physical welfare of His community.

It is as she is thus engaged that Deborah is prophetically inspired to involve herself in matters of warfare. The military leader of her day is a man from Naphtali by the name of Barak. Now, the responsibilities of this office are weighty and constant. The Israelites were under attack by both the eastern Canaanite armies of Jabin and the Philistine forces inhabiting the west coast and intermingling cities. The homeland was dangerous and volatile. The enemy was powerful and extremely well armed. Barak's armies were lumberjacks, farmers, and laborers, armed with axes, crude weapons, and farm implements.

God commanded Barak to fight the armies of Jabin that were amassed on the plain below Mt. Tabor. The forces, commanded by Sisera sported an ominous arsenal of 900 iron chariots with scythes on the axles. Barak was afraid and unwilling to attack.

From her place of judgment between the palms, Deborah learns of Barak's hesitancy to obey God and approaches him in rebuke. She reminds him that he is commanded by God to attack and has been promised the victory. Barak responds by indicating that he will indeed go into battle, but only if Deborah joins him. Deborah goes but not without informing Barak that her support comes with the price tag of the victory being attributed to a woman.

The horrific battle ensues; Sisera is soundly routed by Barak's forces, and flees the battlefield to seek refuge in the tent of a mere woman named Jael. Unfortunately for Sisera, Jael is the wife of Heber, the Kenite, who is a fellow warrior of Barak. Sisera commands Jael to watch at the door of the tent and warn him if Barak's men should approach. She drugs him with warm milk, awaits his unconscious state, and pounds a tent peg into his head. Final victory is realized at the hand of a woman.

Chapter five is a written recording of the traditional victory song or praise offered to God for again preserving His people. It includes *all* of the details; good, bad, and ugly. But, that's the Bible for you.

WHAT WOMEN NEED TO KNOW

I do not have to tell women how powerful we are. Our influence is felt from the hearth to the White House. It is unmistakable and awesome, but with it comes great responsibility. We must take that call seriously. It is a time of preparation. So, wake up! We are asleep in the light, and that is not acceptable. It will be difficult to rise to this occasion, but it is mandatory that we do it now. Those political types who fancy themselves to be much brighter and more capable than the female moral majority are waiting like wolves to devour us. Let them wait. We will be heard, and we will not give up. This is our children's future. This is our nation's future. We are following in the footsteps of the Israelites, whose lineage we share, and that is why we study the life of Deborah. She stood in the face of adversity and led by example and wisdom.

Additionally, the recurring *theme* in the book of Judges should be our warning shot across the bow. If we ignore this history, we *will* repeat it in America. Our kids and grandkids will pay the price, and we will be guilty on all counts.

You see, the problem of moral decline in our great country is *not* the fault of unbelievers. It is the fault of god-fearing, church-going people who are busy being soothed by spiritual Novocain and feel-good doctrines. If we fail to activate, it will be to our great shame and disgust. If we succeed, as I believe we can, it will be our greatest victory. We will not take prisoners, nor can those of you who choose to sit back, assist us, while taking in those saccharine messages of the love of God and ignoring the savory messages of the justice of God. I need a few million strong women out there who are ready to rumble. To begin with, let's take a look at some of the symptoms of the problem.

It has been a few decades since American women were reinforced for their dedication in the home. The message to be vital, career-oriented, and equal to men has been a sounding siren probably since the time of Susan B. Anthony's first call for women's rights. Please do not misunderstand. I am a strong, assertive woman, and we should vote, and speak, and judge, and lead. But, I question those among us who believe that you must *choose* between being a strong woman or a submissive woman. The inherent problem with this kind of thinking is the belief that one choice precludes the other. That we cannot be vital and productive while focusing on homemaking, mothering, and a godly marriage is an insidious lie perpetrated by hateful and angry people.

There. I said it. I know that I have just opened the floodgates, and that I *will* be taken to task for this belief. Oh well, I am aware that I am not a great therapist. Otherwise, I would let the discovery process take its course and the emotional healing begin, insight upon insight. Sorry. That is not my purpose in the writing of this book. But, humor me while I explain that incendiary comment.

I believe that many traditional women will relate to feeling patronized when the feminist movement says something like; "If a woman chooses to be a stay-at-home mom, we truly support her, BUT—"And, it is the *but* that heralds the call to arms, extolling the virtues of the feminist movement, women's rights, and the determination to disallow male domination. The real predicament here is that a majority of women, wives, mothers, and educated professionals, *do not* feel powerless, stifled, or dominated. In fact, the opposite may be true for most of these empowered women who manage homes, families, civic duties, volunteer activities, healthy relationships, ministries, and, often, a career. That is not a startling revelation to the conventional women of today. We know how much power we wield. We do not always wield it with impunity, but we recognize it for what it is.

I know, for example, that the liberal voice tries to appeal to female voters because they see the large support base to be garnered. The problem, as is the case with the majority of liberal pundits, is that they refuse to accept the message that is bombarding them from all sides in countless situations. A truly logical person cannot come to the table with pre-conceived notions and rationally impose those notions upon the data. That is neither good science nor good logic. A viable logistician reviews the data and concludes in support of the facts.

And, the facts clearly indicate that the feminist movement in the form of organizations like NOW is dwindling in their support and membership, while organizations like Concerned Women for America are growing and becoming stronger. The outcome of the 2004 presidential election, in its metamorphosis of ever-expanding red states, was a clear indication of national voice. You can dress it up however you choose and bend the statistics however you wish, but the facts are the facts. America wants morality, a return to traditional values, and a real dialogue concerning the issues. We are tired of filibusters, talking points, rationalizations, grandstand politics, and dirty campaign tactics. We get plenty of this at home with the children as they bicker, name-call, lie, whine, blame, and continually find creative ways of avoiding doing the right thing.

Today's American women want the truth. We want respect. We want worthy husbands, fathers, and leaders who possess integrity. We want a nation that is rabidly protecting an atmosphere that holds life and marriage and such basic values sacred. And, it is becoming more and more apparent that we must step out, behind, in front of, next to, and in spite of men who have given away their God-given calling to the extremely vocal minority.

THE FACE OF TRUE EVIL

And, that brings me to the heroine (and, I hope, prototype) of this literary work. As we begin to study and understand this historical account, it is important to note that the repeating theme of the Book of Judges always begins with: "And the people did evil in the sight of the Lord." Each time a strong and faithful judge died, the slow-learning Israelites slipped into idolatry, wickedness, and the politically correct philosophies of the time. They discarded the admonitions of the Creator God, and did what seemed right in their own eyes. Hey, I did not make this stuff up. It is written in chapter after chapter, each replete with *historical* Biblical accounts, intended to protect us from repeating the mistakes of the past.

Tolerance, personal space, respect for individual morality, acceptance of non-traditional practices and values, deification of the person above the Creator, vilification of the Biblical standard, and a general mood of non-interference are running rampant in the good, old U.S. of A. To be a non-judgmental person is believed to be the zenith of personhood itself. To be tolerant of others beliefs is considered the apex of righteousness. To be accepting of any and all philosophies is thought to be intellectual paradise. These things underpin the liberal agenda and exasperate the moral majority. We are running around doing what is right in our own eyes, without a single compass point for reference. Good grief!

But, surprise! These basic tenets are not extended with the same verve and conviction when being applied to Christian concepts and movements. Take the crosses, nativities, references to God, and all symbols of the love of Christ out of the public square and the unbelievers love it. Now then, if it was left at that, it would be demoralizing and irrational, but the attack does not stop there. Even the activities held sacred inside our churches, homes, and social groups are being infiltrated by those who would sanitize belief in God from every point in the nation.

The term religious right has become a phrase that is spat out like a bad piece of fish whose content somehow just doesn't make the grade. What used to conjure up thoughts of home, family, and box lunches now stimulates talk of purple fruit drink, and fanatical frenzy! They don't like this God of ours. They don't like us judging them. They want to be left to their own personal beliefs, without having to see any depiction of the antithesis anywhere. They are merely doing what is right in their own eyes and wish to be left to it. *We* may not behave that way because we oppose *their* choices and lifestyles. Our opinions and beliefs are not welcome. We have become like historical Israel, in need of a Deborah.

And, so, in order to be considered astute by today's liberal standard, women must be gung-ho for neutralized male-female roles and men must celebrate the apparent equalization, without flinching. What I mean by this is, currently, each of *us* is doing what seems right in our own eyes and would relegate any moralistic watch-cry to the devil. And, the result of this groundswell of individuality seems to be confusion on the part of both sexes. We don't know what is acceptable any more. Women are finding themselves apologizing for *not* working outside the home. And, men don't know if it is permissible to open the darn door for a lady or let it fly in her empowered face!

It has reached epidemic levels as dissatisfaction in our personal lives, families, and country strangle out the last vestiges of hope. I could name several acquaintances, whom I have encountered just this week, who report their life as some kind of repetitious nightmare where getting up, going to work, coming home, and going to bed is their synergy. Women are depressed, stressed, and confused and men are depressed, stressed, and confused. The most popular response now is for men to step aside and wait their turn in the wings. Perhaps Barak, the Israelite captain of the military, was in this esteemed group when Deborah sounded the alarm. It was a time for courage and unflinching decision as the enemy forces advanced against God's people. Ezekiel 22:29–31 explains a similar situation. It reads:

> *The people of the land have used oppressions, committed robbery, and mistreated the poor and needy; and they wrongfully oppress the stranger. So I sought for a man among them who would make a wall, and stand in the gap before Me on behalf of the land, that I should not destroy it; but I found no one. Therefore I have poured out My indignation on them; I have consumed them with the fire of My wrath; and I have recompensed their deeds on their own heads.*

Now, a breached wall was a very big thing in Ancient Israel. Only the bravest of the brave would stand and fortify that place. Many of our country' leaders are cautiously avoiding the disdain of liberal thinkers while leaving the breached walls wide open. It is our time to fortify the wall according to the wisdom of God's Word, no excuses accepted.

So, then, if the men will not stand for the right, the women *will* stand in the gap. People are doing evil in the eyes of the Lord, and our kids will pay the bill. It is truly a time to be Deborah. It is with gratitude and admiration that I share the account of her life with each of you. I write, also, with trembling hope that I will strike a chord with godly women everywhere and motivate the feminine armies who long for the safety and sanity of the blessings of obedience. And, so, let's just get on with the discussion of Deborah, judge, scholar, prophetess, substitute military general, powerful political leader, favored by God and, yes, a woman. Let the hyperventilation begin!

2

Will the Real Judge Stand Up?

"When all that generation had been gathered to their fathers, another generation arose after them who did not know the Lord nor the work which He had done for Israel."

JUDGES 2:10

DEBORAH WAS UNIQUE AMONG the judges of the time. No, it was not unusual for a woman to be in a position of authority. This fact flies in the face of those who would consider the Bible to demean and oppress women. Women lived under many stringent requirements in Old Testament times, but so also did men. God is no respecter of persons and sexuality is not now, nor was it then, excluded. Men were expected to govern themselves by highly rigid rules and standards and were accountable to God, who manifested Himself in a much more obvious manner than He does today, often including pillars of fire and pillars of salt or burning bushes and burning priests. The stakes (no pun, please) were high. Women, in return, were monitored in a similar manner and expected to conform and obey.

Now, that sounds a little harsh and certainly not tolerant. But, that is how it was. To the casual reader of the text, complete with our American expectation for equality, this uncompromising life would seem horrific. What we do not appreciate, without deeper study, is that the culture of the Old Testament also required an ethic of integrity throughout the societal structure that respected, preserved, honored, and protected both men and women. When properly followed, that is the beauty of God's plan. Men were men of integrity and trustworthiness, and women were women of modesty and industry. In most cases, where obedience reigned, life was good. And, like today, when God's kids kicked against the goads, life was miserable.

DEBORAH'S EXEMPLARY OBEDIENCE

It was the duty of the judges of the land to mete out punishment and protection according to the Lord's will and commandments. The rules were clear and concise. The warnings were explained in detail. In fact, there was an attention to detail like no other. Deborah knew the expectations of her office. She did *not* make her own laws from the bench. She did *not* dare to disagree with God. And, she knew her place within the system and what was expected of her. How do I know that? The answer to this question is in the account, itself.

> *"Now Deborah, a prophetess, the wife of Lapidoth, was judging Israel at the time. And she would sit under the palm tree of Deborah between Ramah and Bethel in the mountains of Ephraim. And the children of Israel came up to her for judgment."*
>
> JUDGES 4:4–5

Apparently, as can be seen from a careful reading of the text, Deborah was one of the few judges among all of her peers who *actually* performed all of the duties of a judge. And, it is written that she judged all of the people of Israel from her post under a palm tree. Everyone with a gripe came to Deborah. She was not just a figurehead of representation like many of the judges before, and, unfortunately, after her. She was a worthy representative of God's law. Otherwise, He would have taken her out and the people would *not* have continued to seek her counsel and wisdom.

So, Deborah performed her duties with honor and strength. These are attributes that the liberal women's movement would respect. And, if today's liberals were consistent, they would support her philosophies and beliefs also, even if they did not agree. But, alas, Deborah was a God-fearing conservative! How do I know that? We find the answer, again, in the text.

> *Thus let all Your enemies perish, O Lord! But let those who love Him be like the sun when it comes out in full strength.*
> ***So the land had rest for forty years.***
>
> JUDGES 5:31

Enemies—bad. Rest—good. Deborah fought the enemies of the God of Abraham, Isaac, and Jacob. You know, the God spoken of in that Book you don't like. And, after the battle, the bad guys who hated God were dead while those who loved Him shone like the strength of the sun.

The account of Deborah and Barak begins in chapter 4 of the Book of Judges. The book of Judges relates a series of historical cycles, each of which begins and ends with the death of a judge of Israel. chapter 4 does not deviate from that model. Deborah is introduced as God's emissary, sent to salvage His people, yet again, from themselves. Chapter 4 opens with the words: *"the children of Israel again did evil in the sight of the Lord. So the Lord sold them into the hand of Jabin the king of Canaan."* The people are harshly oppressed for twenty years, causing them to cry out to the Lord for deliverance.

> *"And the children of Israel **cried out** to the Lord; for Jabin had nine hundred chariots of iron, and for twenty years he had harshly oppressed the children of Israel."*
>
> JUDGES 4:3

It is somewhat comforting that the people, indeed, saw their need for salvation. That is to say, the Israelites recognized evil when they experienced it and asked to be delivered. They did not rationalize in any kind of politically correct manner that their current condition was merely the result of a changing and more tolerant environment. The Israelites knew the laws, and they knew the consequences for breaking them. There were no long dialogues whose foundational resolve was whether or not evil existed or if the entire subject was even open for interpretation, based on individual beliefs. The people were in bondage. They were suffering, and they knew that suffering was the result of disobedience to God's laws. That was the end of the discussion. They also knew that they needed a representative to deliver them from evil. It is not the least bit different today in America.

SORRY FOLKS! GOD IS *NOT* A LIBERAL

Oh, my. Where to begin? If you are an angry liberal, I lost you as my audience many paragraphs ago. And, if you have hung on, gritting your teeth until that last statement, this may be the place you relegate this epistle to your reference bookshelf. For those of you who remain, I extend some possible food for thought as it relates to the beginning of chapter 4 of the Book of Judges.

In fact, God *does* instruct us that there is evil in the world.

> *"Because the sentence against an **evil** work is not executed speedily, therefore the heart of the sons of men is fully set in them to do **evil**."*
>
> ECCLESIASTES 8:11

> *"The tree of life was also in the midst of the garden, and the tree of knowledge of good and evil."*
>
> GENESIS 2:9B

> *"**Evil** shall slay the wicked, and those who hate the righteous shall be condemned."*
>
> PSALM 34:21

> *"And do not lead us into temptation, but deliver us from the **evil** one."*
>
> MATTHEW 6:13A

> *"Do not be overcome by **evil**, but overcome **evil** with good."*
>
> ROMANS 12:21

> *"Do not quench the Spirit. Do not despise prophecies. Test all things; hold fast what is good. Abstain from every form of **evil**."*
>
> 1 THESSALONIANS 5:19–22

The Bible even informs us that evil recognizes there is *God* in the world, also.

> *"You believe that there is one God. You do well. Even the demons believe—and tremble!"*
>
> JAMES 2:19

If the pain of life inspired the Israelites to *cry out* to God, Israel must have desired a change of circumstances. They understood real evil and were experiencing great discomfort and oppression. It does not make sense that their salvation would have come in the form of another evil oppressor. The subsequent honeymoon effect would have quickly worn off and hopelessness would have crept in. But, the conclusion of the account of Deborah's reign simply states that the land had rest for forty years. The change wrought must have been an exchange of evil for good. Hence, Deborah was a God-fearing conservative who did as the Lord commanded. That would not be popular in liberal circles today. That interest group prefers to revel in euphemistic rhetoric that re-names and re-emphasizes good and evil according to what is current, popular, and holistically *good* in its own eyes.

The hidden challenge here is to determine what God might approve of today and what He may not. I consider the challenge to be hidden because the constant drone of hypnotic liberal mantras has violated us in classrooms, media, entertainment, and even our churches! It is an exercise of sheer discipline to turn off the anti-God diatribe and focus on why our nation and its people are screaming out for a savior. Nobody is asking for a back-of-the-head disapproval and disdain for a kinder, more merciful and accepting country. Lots of Democrats want a better world. Lots of Republicans want a better world. No genuine American, who is not a lunatic, wants hate crimes, injustice, suffering, inequality, or oppressive elitism. These things are a given. However, in order to create a country of gentile and cooperative folks, to whom or what do we turn for the prototype?

SO, YOU THINK THE CHURCH HAS IT ALL SEWED UP

Walk into most any church in America today and hear a message of God's love and mercy and practically choke on the warm fuzzies. The implication that God is real and may be a little angry is considered to be a message of hatred and divisiveness. We are restricted from crying out for deliverance because that may seem to indicate that we have a problem. I submit that we have a problem. The red states submit that we have a problem. The moral majority submits that we have a problem. Our enemies submit that we have a problem. Our children submit that we have a problem. Our founding fathers would most definitely submit that we have a *problem*.

And yet, the liberal left negates the submissions and points the skinny finger of blame at fanatical Christian demagogues.

The most widely used technique from their camp seems to be to ignore the facts, ignore the voices of the people, and march on into Sodom and Gomorrah! No matter how you dress up disobedience and evil, it will do its damage. Judges, chapter 4, verse 1 states that "—*the children of Israel again did evil in the sight of the Lord.*" They were not miserable because of what *they* considered to be evil, but what *God* considered to be evil. Their deliverer, appointed and called by God, Deborah, righted what was wrong by turning to the Creator God of the universe and following His command. The outcome was forty years of peace. If we, as a nation, indeed desire peace, we may benefit by considering the tried and tested methods followed by the judges of Israel. I choose to study the reign of Deborah because she was a woman, and I speak largely to women because I believe *we* can turn the tide. This is not about equality, career viability, or choices. This is about our nation's future, our children, our peace, and the lack there of.

Now, Deborah judged *all* of Israel. Remember, a study of the accounts contained in the book of Judges indicates that she may have been one of the only judges in Israel to actually perform the duties of a judge. Other judges of the time maintained their positions mostly as figureheads acting as stabilizing influences for peace in the land. The judges were appointed to rescue Israel from oppression and call the people of God to repentance and obedience. Little time was left for civil adjudication or interpretation of the law.

However, the account of Deborah differs significantly from that paradigm. Seated under a palm tree, she received, advised, and determined legal issues for all of Israel. Men *and* women sought her wisdom and judicial consideration on every necessary occasion. She was clearly respected and admired by the Israelite nation. That she was a woman was of no consequence to the people of God who willingly followed her counsel and considered her to be a legal authority. Many commentaries on the subject indicate that women of power were not all that uncommon. Deborah's position did not raise eyebrows or cause mumblings among the people pursuant to her audacity in reigning over women *or* men. There are accounts of women throughout the Old and New Testaments that reveal strong, capable women who changed the outcome of events, led the people to accomplish God's will, and stood as leaders and movers and shakers.

In fact, in the case of Deborah, the powers of her judgeship exceeded the duties of all of the male judges of her time. And as we see later in the account of her reign, she was not too shy to speak out firmly and authoritatively to Barak, the apparent commander in chief of the fighting forces. In fairness, the indication is that the duties of the men were performed by women due to the lack of diligent stewardship on the part of the men. The male leaders had become weak. They lacked focus and faith in God. I will be drawing a parallel often throughout this book between the historical events reported in the book of Judges and those events in today's America.

We live in a time in which our male leaders seem to be bending to political correctness, career aspirations, and polling results. Our churches are soft-selling Jesus in velvet wrappers with puppet shows and *really neat music*. Maintaining marriage vows is considered to be old fashioned and restrictive. The expectation of correct and respectful behavior from our children is believed to be repressive and abusive. Tolerance is the valued watchword on the lips of moral ethicists. Alternative ideas and lifestyles are regarded with greater enthusiasm than are traditional values. Open-ended solutions are taught and modeled.

And very much like the leaders of Deborah's time, our country is teeming with those who would rationalize obvious sin, like adultery, in order to keep intact their political ideologies and maintain their perceived power. I am reminded of those insipid dialogues of several years ago when Americans were trying to "sort out" what was adulterous sex and what was not in order to keep a real pro in the White House.

Without question, the prestigious legal minds of our day would scoff at Deborah's law library. She referenced only the full commands *of* God, the minimum standard of the Ten Commandments, the Mosaic Law, the traditions and ceremonial laws given *by* God, and the substantial and consistent revelation *from* God. Yes, Deborah gave great judiciary weight to pillars of fire, rocks that sprang forth water, compass clouds, salt-encrusted statues, and, oh yeah, the actual presence of God hovering over the mercy seat of the covenantal ark. I think the handicap goes to modern-day attorneys who often rely on law books that have become obsolete before the ink is dry. Don't get me started!

In short, the people are doing evil in the eyes of the Lord while repetitively doing what is right in their own eyes. If ever there was an atmosphere ripe for oppression, this is it. God will not be mocked and He may call upon women to right this downward spiral.

FOR SUCH A TIME AS THIS

In an attitude of sincere and obedient submission to God, it is time for us to become like Deborah so that good, honorable men awaken from their moral lassitude, shake off the drug-like trance of popular opinion, and throw their shoulders into it.

I am extremely hopeful that there is a little Deborah in each of us. Perhaps, I am more determined that there be a *lot* of Deborah in all of us. Godly women today are the victims of role confusion from all sides, stemming from even the counsel of well-meaning religious leaders who work to re-establish healthy, whole families by referring to Biblical passages emphasizing feminine submission or silence. It is a pity that this powerful resource is passed off with such distaste and a foolish determination that has been inspired by the practice of truly lousy exegesis of scripture.

For example, I would not want an assistant who hid his or her talents under the proverbial bushel in order to placate my ego. We neither like nor do we respect "yes men." But, have you ever considered that the willful need to have subordinates agree with and validate a position is just such a job description? Maybe, you might consider it now. In the best sense, leadership is the ability to motivate and appreciate the gifts of those in our charge thereby providing an environment of productivity and peaceful cooperation.

I am not calling for mutiny or disobedient contempt for our God-designed purposes. I only desire to re-visit the facts and consider the possibility that women may indeed be true helpmates in the purest sense of the word. And sometimes, a faithful helpmate must lift or push a faltering mate back into the game. Deborah fulfilled that duty for Barak and stands as an example for the women of America at this pivotal time in *our* history. We can certainly learn from history. It is the wisest among us who learn history's lessons and put the education to positive use. Allow me to explain myself.

I once watched with fascination while a group of preschool children attempted to "dig a hole to China" (their words) in a large, sandy playground. This particular playgroup contained more boys than girls almost by half again. Two boys had garden shovels and sand buckets. One older fellow had a regular shovel. Three of the little girls had kitchen teaspoons and plastic cereal bowls. These last items were not included in the play area, initially. The girls had improvised from the nearby playhouse. Two more boys scooped the sand with their bare hands and pulled great piles of it under their legs and behind them. It was not very long before the physical properties of sand became apparent. As the hole became deeper, the sides caved in and filled their hopes with frustration. The boys responded by digging harder and faster, sand flying and tools bumping each other. This was too much for the little ladies who moved away from the frenzy and watched with disdain.

Upon realizing that the boys were now unsafe to approach, the girls moved to another area several feet away and began to methodically empty a hole with their poor implements. They worked together with relaxed countenances enjoying the feel of the sand and the camaraderie much more than the drive to reach Hong Kong. Eventually, the boys exploded in a sand fight and were escorted to time out. The women's team accomplished the digging of a hole large enough to fit them all, which then became a pretend swimming pool that they all enjoyed.

So that you do not become convinced that I have left our subject matter behind, consider this: If you lose sight of your goal, become immersed in the competitive obsession to win, or lose the rhythm of cooperation, you will fail. And if you fail, someone will commandeer your dream. We can accept the failure to dig a sand pit to China, but we must not allow the dream that built our country to be hijacked by oppressors. It is a foolish man who builds his house upon the sand. I did not make up this illustration, as you know. But, this simple Bible reference is the foundation for the entire message of this book. America is crumbling beneath us. There is a clear solution to the decay. And, it may take an army of single-minded women to point it out. At the least, Christian women can provide the behind-the-scenes support that allows glorious results at the proscenium. However, if we cannot convince the commander to enter the fray, we shall stand at the ready, tent peg in hand and wait for our moment.

A BRIEF HISTORY

There were twelve judges in Israel prior to Samuel. The account of their service is contained in the book of Judges, which outlines the 299-year history from Othniel to Eli. This government of judges was raised up to avenge Israel from their enemies and to purge Israel of their idolatries. As I have already discussed, Deborah was unique in that she performed the actual duties of a judge of Israel. I know many attempts have been made to exegete some explanation for the fact that one of the greatest judges of Israel was a woman. I have heard them all, I think, unless there is some little fellow out there with some new conspiracy theory about Deborah only *dressing up* as a woman. That would just bring other ridiculous suppositions into the argument so I will stick with the currently accepted explanations.

The most supported and salient argument is that the men of Israel were not stepping up and discharging their godly duties, therefore a woman was used by God to get the job done. Okay. I accept that theory, mostly because that is what is happening today all over our nation. Christian men are leaving their homes, wives, children, responsibilities, and spiritual callings en masse. The process of "finding oneself" sounds very much like this quote: *"And the people of Israel did what seemed right in their own eyes."* So perhaps, the weaker vessel was chosen to deliver God's people because the stronger vessel was off doing right in his own eyes. That does not negate the fact that Deborah was wise enough to judge civil and moral concerns among the Israelites, was sought for advice and counsel by the people, and even provided the impetus behind the men of the time, forcing them into action against God's enemies. That is a powerful and vital woman of God. It follows that the women of the church today can be, also. We have the same God, the same commandments, and the whole of scripture.

It may be helpful to provide a brief explanation of what it meant to be a judge in Israel during the time of Deborah and Barak. If you are familiar with the culture of the Old Testament, you know that there were disagreements and legal questions to be settled according to the laws of the time. And if you understand human nature, we might agree that where two or three of God's people are gathered, there lies contention in the midst! (I am aware that the verse does not end that way but this creative adaptation supplies a great illustration of the need for judges.)

The situation was further exacerbated by the fact that the people of Israel had become wanton and secure in their perversions. As we know, one of the greatest strengths the enemy has against God's people is desensitization, or the concept that the deeper we fall into sin, the easier it becomes to dull the conscience. This fact is never more evident than in the horrific slide into deeper depravity that accompanies serial crimes.

And so, evil was abounding in Israel, sin was all around, and Satan was having the time of his dark life!

However, the complications did not end there. Deborah was judging the people in the southwest side of the country that was infested with Philistines, sworn enemies of the Israelite people. More often than not, the roads were vacant because of the people's realistic fear of being harmed. It was even uncommon to see the Israelites freely going to the wells to gather the water that was a critical necessity in the dry, desert land. Going out was risky as was the open profession of their faith.

And so, there sat Deborah underneath her palm listening to diatribe after selfish diatribe about civil disputes, probably suppressing revulsion at the lifestyles and choices of the people, firmly staying true to God's law that stood as her comfort and strength. The Philistines were on the rampage trying to commit jihad against the Israelites and the men of the city were caving in on all sides, just like that preschool sand pit.

But, God does not leave nor forsake His children even in their darkest hours. He will save *His* people in *His* time and according to *His* sovereign will. Now in case you are tempted to become cavalier in your Christian walk, do not forget that Father does not stop short of the woodshed when we are reveling in sin. We reap what we sow. God will see that consequences are meted out. It was the same then as it is now. Nevertheless, God had a plan to free the Israelites from the oppression of Jabin and that plan included a direct attack on the enemy's armies.

Given the environment of fear and perversion, it is not surprising that Barak was not anxious to test God's faithfulness. Of course, God is always faithful, but his people may not always be convinced that they deserve the support. The world was filled with weak men, sinful people, and one lone voice of faith, Deborah. The cycle was repeating itself, yet again, and she stood in a place of responsibility with concern for the outcomes.

It is most likely helpful to consider the kinds of sins with which the Israelites of that day struggled. Knowing their mistakes could after all assist us today in avoiding those same dangers. Also, it allows us an insight into Deborah's concerns and issues. Some of the behaviors included in the culture smacked of direct disobedience to God's laws as well as a more insidious undercurrent of perversion.

The people had been warned of the dangers of inter-marriage with the pagan inhabitants of the land. They ignored the warnings and inter-married. Once those alliances were made, it was a simple step to enter into the worship of idols and the practice of improper private worship. And so, the Israelites placed their faith in improper priests, worshipped Baal and Ashteroh, and participated in lying, stealing, adultery, murder, and sexual perversions. They became a nation *tolerant* of sin and disobedience. As a direct consequence, God became angry and delivered them over to oppression.

An understanding of these ancient objects of worship may produce some insight relating to our current subject matter. You see, I am often perplexed about the attraction created by what seems to be only superstition and illusion. The very fact that the ancient pagan entities were never able to produce anything other than magic tricks leads me to believe that their worship was perfunctory and accepted in place of scholarship, possibly as an excuse for bad behavior. I am also not unaware that the liberal thinkers of our day would include the God of the Bible in this mix. They are simply childish in their research and angry with the truth. That should stir up a few collective neurological strokes.

To continue, the ancient world was, indeed, the first melting pot ever stewed, and so with the blending of tribes and cultures came the metamorphosis of their religious practices and deities. Baal, in fact, was revered by the Phoenicians, the Canaanites, the Philistines, the Moabites, and the never-ending-collection of other "*—ites.*"

As a foundational definition, the name, Baal, means lord, master, or owner. As an object of worship, Baal was considered the god of storms and fertility. The Philistines called him Baal-Zebub. A minor evolution made good an introduction to the god, Beelzebub, the lord of the flies or prince of demons. Most just know him as Satan. In the time of the judges, he wore many hats and does to this day.

This chameleon-like demon was considered by these ancient peoples to be the brother and even consort of the goddess, Ashteroh. She, too, was an eclectic mix of popular deities. She was the Canaanite goddess of war and love, by some considered the queen of heaven. The Asherah poles destroyed by Gideon were images of trees planted to the worship of the goddess of the same name, morphed from the many names. In Egypt, she was Ishtar. To the Sidonians, she was Asherah. The Canaanites also called her Anath or Astarte. For purposes of simplicity, I have used the name familiar to Deborah. Just suffice to say that these distortions were in reference to the same pagan idol. Ashteroh was the feminine side of Baal, or as we know them, Satan and his demons. And, the depths of depravity that were acceptable as a worship offering is legend, even today. *That* is why God gave his people over to oppressors and why he had warned them of the dangers associated in fraternization with the enemy.

ARE YOU TALKING TO ME?

This is the just God of the Bible and not the impotent god many of us have created in our own minds in order to wriggle out of *our* shame. I am well aware that many of the inhabitants of our great land, today, would take umbrage at this simple expression of God's justice. That is of little concern to me. Let the veins pop out in their tiny heads all they want. Anyone with even a limited understanding of the laws of logic must come to the conclusion that if there *is* a God and He *has* revealed Himself in the Holy Scripture, our opinion of what is fair and merciful has no bearing on God's decisions. The lack of respect for the Lord shown by the Israelite people during the time of Deborah did not rescue them from their terrible oppression, either.

Any nation that ignores the commands of a Holy God *will* suffer the consequences. Lest you think that God cannot raise up another nation to bring His plan to fruition, please refer to the account of the life of King Saul. Or, let's pause for a reflection on the implosion of Solomon. Do you recall that he was the son of David, known for his God-given gift of great wisdom? We could say that he was the wisest man, ever, I think. He built the most beautiful of temples, was rich beyond all imaginable fantasies, and is the model for judicial wisdom. Do you know what brought about his destruction? Solomon was punished by the Lord for his worship of, you guessed it, Ashteroh, and Chemosh, and Molech, all of which was preceded by his unholy relationships with foreign women.

He "loved" the daughter of the Pharaoh, worshippers of Ishtar, the women of the Moabites, worshippers of Chemosh, the women of the Ammonites, worshippers of Molech, and the women of the Edomites, Sidonians, and Hittites, those who worshipped their own personal versions of Ashteroh. The wisest man, *ever*, took the oldest bait *ever*. Who do we think *we* are? America is *not* the land of promise without the parameters created by Our Father God. We can be replaced. Don't forget that.

So, just imagine a day in the life of Judge Deborah. She most probably began her day with devotions and a simple meal of bread and meat. God had His hand on her and so the spirit must have been revealed in her life and her heart. Therefore, even in darkness, I think Deborah felt empowered. The closest I can come to what that must have felt like would be participation in deeply worshipful services with my church family. Sometimes the fellowship of God is palpable. Deborah was focused and that assumption is based on her coming behavior.

Deborah dressed and went to the place of judgment. Some say that this was under a palm tree in the open air. Other commentaries indicate that the court was in a building by the palms. It really doesn't matter because the people of God knew where to find her. She was there because she was faithful to her calling. She was there because she knew what was at stake. And, she was there because God strengthened her arm, and her mind, and her will in order that she could perform the mammoth task of seeing to the rescue of her people in direct submission to her God.

Liberal women's groups today would consider her effort to be a great waste because Deborah took her direction from that mean, old Christian God who requires us to follow the rules—His rules! She would get an 'atta girl" for her strength and a raspberry for her beliefs. Some serious tongue clicking belongs here.

To continue with the account, Deborah seated herself in the judge's chair and began to unravel the stories and complaints of the Israelites and apply the law to the conclusions. She did not make things up as she went along. She did not bow to the popular opinion of the day. She was not preoccupied with the notion that things had changed since the ancient times of Abraham and Moses. She had *not* come a long way, baby. Deborah applied *the law* and went home. I am sure that her decisions were not too popular and that she would be filibustered to death in today's America. Remember, the people were doing what seemed right in their own eyes and God was not pleased! Their oppression was a result of their sin and not their genuine desire to please God. He does not like that.

As Deborah judged and exercised her faith, the oppressors continued in their belief that they would always triumph over these silly Israelites. And, that is where Barak becomes pivotal to the plan because many of God's people were sick and tired of the oppression and were crying out to the Lord for deliverance. That was their way. Thankfully, the people who desired a return to the safety and peace of obedience were becoming a majority voice in the country. Prayers were prayed. Worship was humbly presented and God, in His mercy, sought to deliver

His children. The chosen vessel was Barak, the leader of the armies. Only one hitch existed in the strategy. Barak lacked the faith that he needed to overcome his fears and limited understanding to go boldly, into battle. Enter our heroine.

Now remember, the atmosphere of the time was one of compromise. The Israelite people had become un-equally yoked in pagan relationships against the express command of God. It does not require rocket science to grasp the concept that we become like those with whom we fellowship. In other words, we become a disciple of our peers. That should cause some sober thoughts for parents about the friends of their children, the schools attended by their children, and the media playground in which their children tarry. I am well aware that some of you are already mouthing phrases like: not my kids, or not *our* schools, ad nauseum. And, that brings me to my next exasperated plea.

Please disciple your kids with Believers. I don't want you to indoctrinate them and pasteurize everything they learn. I want you to educate them, strengthen them in the fear and wisdom of the Lord, and then turn them loose to answer God's calling on their life. If your kids are wild-eyed in front of the X-box, power-blitzed by a liberal, secular humanist teacher, or hanging around that nice atheist boy down the street, see the optometrist. Or, better yet, read the Book of Judges. You need your spiritual eyesight checked.

Forgive my straight talk and go out and do the investigations necessary to assure that your kids are growing up godly. Leave your ill-conceived notions and rationalizations behind and get the facts. You may be quite surprised by the sheer quantity of compromise thrown at your precious little ones every moment by the bucketful. Then, go and find a good Christian school and excuse my soapbox moment.

After years of history and dump trucks full of longitudinal studies, we know that our choice of spouse determines our future success and happiness. God knew it first. He continued to warn His people throughout the Old and New Testament of the dangers of fraternizing with the enemy. He *continued* to warn them because they *continued* to ignore the warnings. There must have been a really awesome mote and beam salesman in town selling armloads of regrets to the Israelite people. The account informs us that after the Israelites married pagans, they began to compromise their very beliefs, immediately. America has plenty of compromising citizens, which is why we are having this conversation.

In addition to the compromises resulting in un-holy marriage alliances, the children of Israel began to worship false gods, idols, and their own inclinations above the admonition of the Father of us all. They began to comport themselves much like horses whose corral has been inadvertently opened. The farther they get from the safety of the boundaries, the more disoriented, unruly, and vulnerable they become. As the supreme creation of our God, we have proven to be voracious in our perversions the farther we get from the protection of our faith. Therefore, it was a minute step for the Israelite people, through their utter desensitization to the truth, to abandon all that was holy for all that was not. They apostatized from their faith, left their beliefs in disarray, and opened themselves up for oppression and ruin.

Now, let's see. Does any of this ring a bell, strike a chord, or proudly wave from the flagpole? American politics today is a kind of awkward dance wherein the participants try to sneak up on their opponents, make large and loud accusations, pummel everyone off point, and name-call until all participants have forgotten that we have a founding document which can clarify all. The Constitution of the United States was created by deeply Christian men within the will of God to provide the foundation and the boundaries for the greatest country in the world. We did not get to be the world's only super power through the vehicle of compromise.

Now, if my liberal audience begins to experience rage seizures at these suggestions, I would invite them to view exhibit A: Iraq or any other country oppressed by a tyrannical government, and determine if they would like to pursue citizenship there. America is a unique and blessed country allowing freedoms unknown by those in other lands. We are dangerously close to implosion and will experience it if our leaders cease to heed the Biblical warnings.

THE SAGA CONTINUES

What followed in the account of the Israelite people was the rapid decline into oppression and despair. I am reminded of the hundreds of teenagers I have taught over the years who share a similar attitude about sin. Intellectually, they may see the connection between the account of the Israelite tumble into depravity, chronicled in the book of Judges, and a self-same danger, contemporarily. However, each young lad or lady stubbornly believes that they are immune. It will not happen to me, they cry.

I am different, they retort. I can handle it, they resolve. They'll get theirs, I promise. Without a deliverer, God's people would have faced certain destruction and sure grief. The pernicious self-talk of Barak kept him from answering God's call and required a courageous rebuke, but not without the wailing and whining of repentance as a backdrop.

The people realized their hopeless condition and cried out to the Lord for deliverance. Firm resolutions were made, promises were lifted up, and copious tears were wept. Over and over the people cried out. And all the while Deborah sat, juxtaposed in the palm tree vicinity, between Ramah and Bethel, in the hill country of Ephraim, calmly listening to God. It was as she was thusly engaged that she received notification from God that Barak was not responding to the Lord's commands.

3

Are We There Yet?

"Lord, how they have increased who trouble me!
Many are they who rise up against me.
Many are they who say of me,
'There is no help for him in God.'
But You, O Lord, are a shield for me,
My glory and the One who lifts up my head.
I cried to the Lord with my voice,
And He heard me from His holy hill."

PSALM 3:1–4

I THINK WE CAN all identify with anyone who may feel bullied by a practical and fearful personal reality and then begin questioning his or her hope in Christ. I, for one, am not always certain that God will come through in time to save me from my oppressors, or worse, myself. This is the very situation that may keep us from effusively expressing disagreement with the leaders of our country. We are like Barak, shrinking in fear from nine-hundred, figurative, iron chariots while God patiently awaits our obedience.

It is at this defining moment that Deborah arrives on the scene to scold, rebuke, and motivate Barak into battle. He did not want to go and she could not lead the army. It is unlikely that Deborah was even battle-worthy. The strength of her demeanor must have been shored up only by her faith and the sure knowledge that God would do what He had promised. Facing the well-armed Canaanite army was a terrifying event. It seems now to have been a suicidal notion.

I can relate to Deborah's "I'll–die-trying" attitude. This is how I feel when I write my congressman. The density of the wasteland of twisted logic and rationalizations surrounding our government is epic. Often, a rational suggestion becomes smothered by extremely vocal, liberal demagogues whose screams of inclusion and tolerance are drowning out the weak cries of the compassionate conservatives beneath the huddled mass.

What happens next in chapter four of Judges is the event that causes a twinkle in the eye of Christian women everywhere, and a downward glance from the men. Barak informs Deborah that the only way he will go into battle is if she goes with him. Funny? I don't think so. Could it be contemporarily relevant? Certainly.

The relevance of the issue is obvious to any mother who has wondered why a legislator cannot make a simple law protecting the unborn without dressing the proposal up with special interest enticements. The right thing to do is always fraught with threatening overtures and complexities. That is, unless the litmus test comes from the Word of God and then, simplicity reigns. Unborn children must be protected at any cost. If the current government cannot get that, perhaps a delegation of modern-day Deborahs must go into the halls of Congress and see to it. Or, what if elected officials had to deal with a huge coalition of women who assert their righteous intent at the ballet box? H-m-m-m.

To assure the deliverance of God's people, Deborah then proposes the parameters surrounding the coming victory. She informs Barak that she will go, but that the consequence of his reticence will be his shameful acceptance as the victory is attributed to a woman. Guess what? He said yes.

She went, and the battle was fought and won by Barak's forces, culminating in the routing out of Sisera, the commander of the Canaanite troops. Every one of the enemy soldiers fell by the sword of the Israelite army. Running for his life, Sisera sought a safe harbor in the tent of another woman, Jael who subsequently gave him drugged milk and tent peg in the head. One must reckon with women like that.

FUTURE OR PAST?

Now I am not suggesting that Christian women storm the Capitol with warm milk and tent pegs. I am however suggesting that we come to a full stand while instructing our government's performance. There are lots of us. We know what is right in the eyes of God. And, it is time to stimulate activity. Blah, blah, blah is no longer an adequate response to the needs of this nation and our children's future. Substance is demanded in the halls of justice. Obedience is commanded in the hearts of God's people.

We are being daily oppressed by the rabid left agenda that would rather see babies sucked from their mother's bodies than snail darters disturbed in the rivers of the desert. God help us!

Real terrorists aggressed our shores, murdered almost three thousand of our citizens, and we are engaged in some type of Kindergarten rhetoric about who hit whom first. I am sorry if I sound inappropriately angry and intolerant but, dear sisters, when will this insanity end? We live in the greatest country on the planet Earth, and we sit with pious and supercilious expressions, awaiting permission to deliver our land. Deborah would not be amused.

This presents a great opportunity to explore the ways in which women may be instrumental in the legislative process. I think this highly charged suggestion could be construed to be like tossing boy-scout water (gasoline) on a campfire. Perhaps we need only a return to the conversations of our founding mothers pursuant to how the First Lady should involve herself in Washington politics to provide direction today.

Initially, James Madison's wife, Dolly, suggested an active part for herself. She began the tradition of White House entertaining and, in so doing, brought us ice cream. God love her! But, the part of hostess will be played by extroverted wives no matter what house they manage. Deeply felt regrets from a fancy party gone awry simply pale in comparison to the wail of suffering that emanates from a formerly free country that has gone awry.

While the part of hostess is traditionally foisted upon Mrs. President, the girls of the White House were and are much more vital. Anna Eleanor Roosevelt traveled, extensively with her husband, Franklin, becoming his eyes and ears after polio struck. She held press conferences, gave lectures and was a spokesperson for the United Nations. Jacqueline Lee Bouvier Kennedy worked tirelessly to make the White House a museum of American history for all of us to enjoy. She was active in charities and supported progress in education and health improvement for the nation's children. Nancy Davis Reagan was and still is committed to the continued success of drug programs that teach our kids to "say no." Rosalynn Smith Carter attended Cabinet meetings, served as a personal emissary to Latin America, and works for human rights and peace. Barbara Pierce Bush serves on the Foundation for Literacy and is a staunch advocate for volunteerism. And, Laura Welch Bush is an honorary Ambassador to the U.N. pertaining to worldwide literacy, champions Early Childhood programs, and serves as a volunteer to important youth initiatives. We've come a long way. We can most certainly go the distance.

The Book of Judges reiterates in its successive accounts of each new judge and deliverer the dangers of ignoring and disobeying God's commands. If, in fact, our country is in the throes of a spreading "I" infection, *we* must seek the cure and apply it to the effected area. Obviously, it is imperative that the diagnosis process be tackled before the correct medication is applied.

In the case of Barak's hesitancy to lead a battle charge, the problem was exacerbated by what I am sure he considered respectful fear. Remember, the Israelites were under the oppression of the Canaanite government and suffered the constant threat of Philistine aggression. We are, in America, free to roam about the country with limited restraint. So, are we really that far gone?

Recently, the issue of whether or not to send money for body armor, food, ammunition, clothing, medicine, support staff, gasoline, armored vehicles, aircraft, boots, helmets, candy bars, towels, soap, paper, and dozens of necessities to protect and care for our soldiers in harm's way in Iraq, was considered by our Democratic congress. President George W. Bush, acting on the requests of the generals on the ground, submitted a funding bill and awaited the outcome. So did our troops.

I ask you, mom, if your son or daughter needed a warm coat, would it take you months to supply it? That is a nauseating thought. But, the legislators who were elected *by* us don't like the war. I don't like seafood, but I realize that the sea is full of it. Anyway, the razor-sharp intellect of our congressional employees led them to microphone after microphone to expound on the morality of the war and the costs thereof. Finally, after many wasted weeks of insipid debate, that selfsame congress submitted a bill to our President that included cute, little earmarks intended to placate the voters back home.

Earmarks is such a precious label, isn't it? It sounds all down homey and bath tubby. But, it simply means that pork barrel spending, pet projects, state-sponsored revenue waste, top-heavy administrative salaries, and the like were "taped on" to the bill so that the President's signature passed the whole lot into law. When I was a kid, our little sisters and brothers were always sent to ask mom and dad for stuff we knew we couldn't have.

You know, ask mom if you can have a cookie, and then just throw in seven more for us.

But then, to make the practice even more unpalatable, in the case of the troop funding request, the congress threw in a pinch of blackmail. The esteemed body waxed philosophical on the proposal that the money for our troops could not be made available at such short notice *unless* its request was attached to these little earmarked projects, already drafted and ready to go. If only we could find a special interest group to lobby for cold kids in trenches, perhaps this kind of hostage crisis could be avoided in the future. I don't know. It sounds like a nice project for women of valor or a great thought to take into a voting booth.

Hey! Foul, you cry! This process has been going on for years. The Democrat-controlled Congress does it. A Republican-controlled Congress has done it. Look, during the drafting of our founding documents, even bad things like slavery were used as bargaining chips (or threats, depending on how you see it) in the approval process. What is the big deal, now?

Clearly, we have forgotten the premise of this part of the book. The discussion is centered on whether or not the United States of America has fallen into egregious sin, filthy enough to warrant comparison to the Israelite-Canaanite conflict of the 12th century B.C. Special interest enticements folded like secret origami into a proposed bill certainly do not rise to the level of disobedience to God's commands, right?

Well, you know how Jesus would often answer a question *with* a question? I am in no way as wise as Jesus. But, I'd like to give the method a try. Why do our legislators not present their pet projects in daylight in their own little envelope? Are they too busy? Is the request just not that big of a deal? Do they desire to save paper and protect the environment? I apologize. There were five questions. But, shouldn't we get an answer to those questions before we pass another creative spending bill? Oops! That was another question.

You see, I am a teacher, and I believe that requests that affect the whole class should be shared with the whole class. Clandestine information is usually kept out of direct light for a reason. Often, the publishing of that information could stimulate a negative response. *We* the people may not agree with *Them*, the personally benefited. In fact, it is highly suspect that earmarks may fund projects that Americans may oppose on the basis of morality, or cost-effectiveness, or down-right stupidity. Don't you want to know?

HOW BAD IS IT?

Just to ground us in the understanding of how sin may work in the heart of a person who rationalizes behaviors, consider the tendency we all have to avoid uncovering the truth in a relationship. If money is missing from our purses, it is sometimes more comfortable to let it go instead of confronting our teen-aged daughter. If suspicious receipts are turning up in our husband's pant-pockets, the trash can is often a quicker fix than conversation. And, since this is possibly uncomfortable territory, let us switch back to a Congress that is hiding information from us. Don't ask, don't tell is already a foundational tenet of our government. It is time for an accounting. It is time for a conversation. It is time to honor our calling from God.

In order to appreciate our present circumstance and identify how far we have regressed, it may be helpful to provide fodder for debate. In October of 2007, a court in Maine voted in favor of allowing schools to give birth control to middle school girls as young as eleven without the consent of their parents. A college in Florida hands out condoms to all of its new students on campus at the beginning of each school year. In Illinois, a local atheist wants the practice instituted by their schools to allow a moment of silence at the beginning of the day to be discontinued. I think the lawsuit was filed because the practice is considered to be a time that thoughts of prayer or God may sneak into the curriculum.

Another great American recently filed suit to disallow the mention of God by veterans during flag-folding ceremonies at the funerals of fallen soldiers. A young grandson of one of our war heroes was presented with a memorial statement that omitted his grandfather's homage to God intended as a part of an honor flag tradition. To be fair, that one was corrected because the people (that's us) complained. Even though I could continue this dubiously esteemed list of symptomatic sin, why don't you sleuth out the accomplishments of your own state's courts and congress and see if they are doing what seems right in your eyes?

I would be lax in my endeavors if I did not include a few tidbits of cultural news to underscore our need for attention to the political climate in America. With every click of the family remote control, the effects of these events expand into our culture like the ripples in a pond. Before we know it, all is lost.

In New York, a mother pushing her baby in a stroller was caught shoplifting by a store security team. When mom realized her plight, she had no other choice. She threw herself on the mercy of the officers, all the while protecting her cherished infant from the scene, right? Sorry, but thank-you for playing. The mother fled the store and left her child behind to fend for herself. Isn't that sweet?

This last Halloween, costume companies found that the more slutty the costume, the better it would sell. This year the companies extended the thrill of looking like a street-walker to pre-teens, who are the fastest growing consumer market. Here is what is really special. Moms and dads are buying them up so as not to disappoint little Brandy, Stormy, Candy, or Brittany and off they go to their first mixer.

Last week, among the several news stations that I joyfully monitor, there were four hilarious stories about pre-teens who have charged hundreds to their cell phones by text messaging their way through history class. Just for fun, wouldn't you love to see what punishment is doled out by the parents? And, oh yes, I have heard all of the white noise conversation about how giving cell phones to our kids keeps them safe and in touch with good old mom and dad in times of need.

Conversely, I have also noticed the rash (no pun intended) of nude photos of our kiddies' classmates published on the internet or sent to countless fave fives throughout the country, all of which were candidly captured by a pre-pubescent cell phone. I can't help but question the motivation experienced by some of the parents of today who agonize over which hand-held device named after a juicy fruit to bestow upon their non-discerning offspring.

While I am injecting personal ideals on the cultural cancers of our day, allow my personal commentary on the dangers of exposing our children to today's media. I will expand on this concept in a later chapter. But, for now, it seems expedient to mention the clear emotional and psychological harm inflicted on a three or four-year-old mind, nestled in front of the family DVD player spewing filth and violence into their home. I have children in my childcare who have seen every PG-13 and R-rated movie that has been released during their short lives, often without the benefit of popcorn. The general response from parents when faced with this kind of criticism is a casual comment containing one or more of the following rationalizations: "I know what's best for my child." "They don't watch that all the time." "It's not like they don't see worse on the nightly news." "Who cares what my child watches?" And, this one is my personal favorite: "If they don't watch it at home, they will see it somewhere else without me to comfort them." I am reminded of this passage in the Book of Romans:

> "—because, although they knew God, they did not glorify Him as God nor were thankful, but became futile in their thoughts, and their foolish hearts were darkened."
>
> ROMANS 1:21

So if it is really all that bad, what's there to do? Truly, *anything* would be better than nothing. Right now, you should be emitting the same disgruntled sigh that you automatically produced when we studied the in-action of Barak on the battlefields of Canaan. As believers in the Most High God, it is our calling to warn the people, rebuke the hesitant sinner, and motivate the reticent warriors. With the profound and faithful advice of Deborah, Barak's forces scrambled down the side of Mount Tabor armed only with crude weapons and clubs to route out the occupation forces seated on nine-hundred chariots with sharp scythes mounted on their axles.

We know how the account of Deborah and Barak ends, and we see that the skirmish brought forty years of peace. The people of God were again forgiven and blessed. And the message clearly resounds that, if the strong will not bow the knee, God *will* use a weaker vessel to confound, confuse, and conquer the mighty. I am only hoping to rally the troops. It is God who designs the victory, lest any one of us take the credit. I do know that God's people will be given the strength to drive in the peg. Still not convinced? I am still not finished.

4

Please Don't Repeat

"Thus let all Your enemies perish, O LORD!
But let those who love Him be like the sun
When it comes out in full strength."

JUDGES 4:31

IMAGINE THAT THIS is just about the time for most of you to engage your back pedals and commence the oral arguments *against* my assertion that things are just as bad today. You are formulating your recitations and pleading *for* a calmer rhetoric that soothes and minimizes our blemishes. If you have liberal leanings, "Good morning on this, your usual day!" But, if you are a conservative, "In the name of all that is reasonable, wake up!" The last thing we need in America, at this critical time, is more hypnotic suggestion. It is time to guard against the *"Wizard of Oz"* syndrome that allows us to ignore the facts and "pay no attention to the man behind the curtain."

Remember that I intimated that we are in jeopardy of repeating the past. Since the *past* we are discussing is the chronicle of events in the book of Judges, we should go there now and do a little comparison shopping, thereby assuring ourselves that the call to alarm is, well, not that alarming. As I promised, I would like to focus on any similarities in our country to the Israelite experience at the time of the Judges. Let me just remind you of the problem:

1. The Israelites did evil in the sight of the Lord and began to serve other gods.
2. God became angry and delivered them up to oppressors.

3. The Israelites cried out for help and God raised up a judge to deliver them.
4. The judge brought peace, but the nation returned to sin as soon as the judge died.

Now then, I have no intention to pour salt in your wound, but just for the sake of clarification, allow me to recount what "doing evil in God's sight" might mean. It might mean, for example, that the people were breaking a commandment or two (thousand). I apologize for the scare. How about if we narrow the discussion field down to a study involving just a few of the Biblical rules?

The message in the Book of Judges indicates that, "—the people were doing what seemed right in their own eyes." It went as follows:

1. The people became un-equally yoked and inter-married with the local pagans.
2. They adopted the pagan worship of Baal and Ashteroh.
3. They began to recognize improper priests.
4. They created improper, private, worship sanctuaries.
5. Lying, stealing, adultery and murder were condoned.

Picky, picky, picky! What in the world are we saying, here? Do I really mean that this narrow and strictly enforced set of errors somehow applies to twenty-first century America? Certainly, the focus of this work is not to convince through brilliant lecture. I'll leave that to the cable news pontificators. But, to be consistent in our thinking and responsible for our own behavior is a sign of maturity and integrity which *is* what I would like to accomplish.

As I have stated, the purpose of this book is to begin a dialogue among God's people that may lead to a day of deliverance for our country and a time of peace for our children. Looking back on the sufferings of the Israelite people as they played hide and seek with God will illustrate a certain pattern that is either worth repeating or valuable to avoid.

Problematic to this discussion is the incensed resistance that is experienced when there is even a slight mention that America is veering wildly into traffic instead of progressively climbing the pyramid of self-actualization. I contend that we are in trouble and the secular progressives want me to shut up. And so, in the spirit of acquiring a battle plan if you are a liberal or for the purpose of jump-starting some forward-moving momentum for Christian conservatives, allow me to compare historical facts.

LET'S REVIEW

As they dwelt in the land of the Canaanites, the chosen people of God were given the benefit of His instruction and its application to their protection and blessings. True to the human nature in us all, the people were irritated, even angry with their Creator because of His seemingly cruel and prohibitive laws. They could not ally themselves with a God who restricted inclusion of all human desires and experiences, no matter how perverse or harmful they were. This God of their fathers had insisted that His children not fraternize with the enemy. Even today in a time of war, this kind of activity could be considered treasonous. Additionally, even though God did not and does not need to explain reasons for His requirements, the Israelite people began to see God as a mean and prejudiced despot. Surely, God could understand that the command not to inter-marry with the Canaanites was just simply the result of an archaic temper tantrum.

Further, the instruction was really much more restrictive in its entirety and referred to a great deal more than the marriage bed. The Israelite people were to keep themselves apart from all of the pagan beliefs, both spiritual and civil. Therefore, the social, interpersonal, spiritual, religious, and governmental mores of the Canaanite community were forbidden territory for the Israelites. God was not concerned about the clothing styles, the food preferences, or the architecture, or any cultural nuances outside of those things that clearly stimulated immoral behaviors. God *was* concerned that His children would become hypnotized by sinful, self-aggrandizing rituals and ideas. Since God created the hearts and minds of His children, He knew full-well the capabilities of their perversion and the damage to be done by following that path. It is of no small import that the idol worship enjoyed by the people of Canaan was typically hyper-natural and could be adjusted to meet the current needs of the worshiper and the expedience of the situation.

In other words, these gods were made in the image of the worshipers, inculcated with flexible characteristics, and lifted up in gyrational ritual whenever the thrill was gone. This would allow the people to do whatever seemed right in their own eyes without the interruption of some pesky god who required a functional conscience. If, in fact, there was no foundational truth, then all was fair in love, war, and life. Today, we call that concept tolerance, progressive thinking, and personal freedom. We hear such insipid comments as: "What's right for you may not be right for me," or "You just can't legislate morality," or "Don't judge me. That is not acceptable." Even my elementary level logic students would respond with umbrage at the ridiculously inconsistent and arbitrary nature of these comments.

Such philosophical suicide is legion in our country, and we stand back with our prayer eyes closed hoping for a new outcome to an old error. We might just as well cross our fingers behind our backs and pretend to be truthful. For the love of God, we must pray! But, let's not fool ourselves with some sodium-pentathol induced trance that, if we hold our breath long enough, the bad men will all go away and all will be well once again.

God told the Israelites to stand for right, to denounce false idols, to shun those who did evil in His eyes, to fellowship with those who loved Him, to follow His commands, and to obey the tribal league from the house of their fathers. It was not just that the children of the Israelites were not to marry the Canaanites. They were not to fellowship with them, worship with them, participate in business with them, follow their customs, or tolerate their oppression.

The terminology "un-equally yoked" means that every time you must perform any activity whose purpose is to propel you forward in any way, you must not be impeded by a destructive and opposing stranglehold. God had and has a plan for each of His children. Doing it His way brings peace. Doing what seems right in our own eyes brings oppression. You do the math.

Okay. I am trembling from the explosive energy being thrust right now into the universe by the liberal secularists and pointed toward my humble self. They are no doubt convinced that I am evil incarnate and are faint with disbelief. I respectfully request that they hang around for the big finish, but I am quite certain that the experience would harm them, irreparably as the strong language and firm convictions are akin to a belief in capitol punishment and the right to bear arms. Just remember that this is an historical account of the actual events from the Book of Judges in the Bible. Yes. *I* am drawing a comparison. *I* am not God. I merely report to Him on a regular basis. And, I take names. *I* hope you know that *I* am kidding now.

The Israelite nation had come through a lot prior to the events recorded in the Book of Judges. This is important because we must see through the lens of the time period. If you are a student of history, you know that the veritable cradle of civilization or Mesopotamia had spawned the generations and people groups we know as ancestral to our world today. If you are a student of the Bible, you know that the beginning of human history goes back much farther than Sumeria.

IT IS TRULY RELATIVE

So, enlightened historians, please bear with the mundane details of creation, Adam and Eve, the worldwide flood, the dispersal of the descendants of Noah, the exile and slavery at the hands of the Egyptians, the 40 years of wandering in the desert of modern-day Saudi Arabia, and the tumultuous entrance into the promised land of Canaan. The people of God had been through hell and back, squared.

As members of the human race, we can all relate to the stresses of life, the ravages of war, and the loss of loved ones, poor health, dashed hopes, broken dreams, and the successes and failures of our condition. The United States of America has been through a revolutionary war fought in a strange, new land, a civil war where enmity among families was common, floods, earthquakes, hurricanes, two world wars, financial ruin and depression, terrorism, the creaks and groans of government in flux, carpetbaggers, homesteaders, the gold rush, war babies, baby boomers, generation X, and the new moniker being bantered about for the new generation, the Super Predators, to name a few. We are familiar with challenges.

But, just like the Israelites in the land of Canaan, we have always held to the moral high ground, foundationally shored up by the Creator of us all. The majority of the Western world follows some type of Christian system. America was founded by a Christian majority and based on the continued belief that God did indeed bless us. It is with this experiential history that the events of the life and times of Deborah are understood and embraced by today's woman.

The wives and mothers of Israel had lost husbands and children, suffered through famines, plagues, slavery, religious and civil persecutions, been forced out of their homes, subjected to abuses, molestations, beatings, starving, wars, and, all at once, experienced or been taught about the miracles of God including appearing and disappearing water, manna, fire, salt, instant water corridors, healings, deliverance, the rise and fall of great and godly prophets and leaders, the Ten Commandments, children born to barren women, and hundreds of otherwise unexplainable phenomena.

We are the same. We rise to the same occasions and fall to the same tricks. It is our birthright. It is in our DNA. We are neither better nor any worse than they. We follow in the steps they have trod. Therefore, arrogantly judging their errors is pointless. But, studying their errors and creating a new victory is not. God told the Israelites not to be un-equally yoked. They went right out and got themselves an irregular yoke at the bargain agora and hitched it up right nice. Oppression fell swiftly and terribly. What to do?

Let's say that God recommends marriage between one man and one woman. How do we analyze this? I mean, this is America! Let freedom ring and all that, right? I know, let's re-name the sacred institution to include "civil unions." That should do it. No? This kind of exclusionary prejudice is steeped in the bile of the tolerant. True liberals want the re-definition of marriage to include homosexual, bisexual, polygamous, sodomitical, and any other creative coupling that can be imagined. As a judge in Israel, Deborah knew and adjudicated pursuant to these very kinds of perversions that were occurring in the hill country of Ephraim.

How about your opinion? Do you fall somewhere in between traditional marriage and civil unions? If you even answered that question without a defined reference to the laws of God, please keep reading. I hope to exorcise your demons. Deborah quoted the Old Testament Book of Genesis and ruled thusly on the subject of marriage: For it is written,

> *"Then the rib which the Lord God had taken from man*
> *He made into a woman, and He brought her to the man.*
> *And Adam said: This is now bone of my bones*
> *and flesh of my flesh; She shall be called Woman,*
> *because she was taken out of Man."*
>
> GENESIS 2:22–23

The scripture continues:

> *"And they were both naked,* **the man and his wife,**
> *and were not ashamed."*
>
> GENESIS 2:25

In the nineteenth chapter of Matthew, verses 4–10, Jesus quotes the same passage, affirming that, indeed, one man and one woman doth a marriage make.

Case closed. The legislature in your state is not so succinct. In fact, our country is overwhelmed with political satraps who run like scalded dogs back to their constituency pleading the need for more money, more tolerance, and less righteous pressure. It's a new world, they say. Give a little, take a little, they say. Hey, we all make mistakes, they say. We have to get along, you know. Bi-partisan support is what's important. Business as usual is the tactic de jour.

Not surprisingly, the result is that our government is more about character assassination, finger-pointing, flip-flopping, deal-making, junkets, racism, rhetoric, and lively, but imprecise debate. In short, the government is doing what seems right in their eyes and doing evil in the eyes of God. Oh, boy. Here we go. The gauntlet is thrown and the maze of relative truth must now be traversed.

THERE IS MORE TO THE STORY

God said we must not be un-equally yoked. Traditional marriage is not the only concept waiting to have its fingers and toes removed. Additionally, America is not to ally itself with pagans, murderers, immoral governments who would cannibalize their own people, countries that creep along the ground while feral terrorists slink into their towns and imbed with their families to kill, steal and destroy, or megalomaniacs who espouse the destruction of any world community that does not agree with their blood atonement or the holy calling given them by their personally created god and maniacal thirst for power.

And, America is not to duck its head, tuck its ears and refuse to make eye contact in calm submission to aggression on our own shores where three thousand of our moms, dads, and children were exterminated by holy war psychopaths. If you find yourself suddenly screaming at the inanimate pages of this work, get thee to a yoke salesman and find comfort in a tolerably equal model. If you are a little indignant and have begun to sense steaminess just beneath the epidermis, the yoke you want is easy and the burden has been promised to be light.

The Israelites committed herem according to God's will. It is not my problem if that offends you. In case that terminology is new to you (it was to me), herem is a Hebrew term that is best translated to mean uncompromising devotion without the possibility of recall or redemption. As the Israelite people came into Canaan, they were commanded to commit herem, and leave nothing alive that breathes. Frightening! But, you and I do not know *exactly* what lay in the hearts and minds of the Canaanites now, do we? And, the Lord God did know and saw the future of His people as they became hopelessly fettered in the spider web of idolatry and perversion that was just life in the big city.

The common American does not understand this concept, but we continue to lower our standards in order to allow for acceptance of all things contrary to the laws of God in our country. After all, we have to live here and get along. We have to welcome all comers to our shores and stand up for personal freedoms no matter who is trampled upon in the fray. We seem to be unequally yoked with ourselves or our philosophies or our co-dependant need to appear nonplussed by any and all abuses of the system or the rules.

The liberal left says that the Constitution is a living document that continues to take on a life of its own even if that means amending it into an impotent scratch pad in order to enable secular progressives to do what is right in their own eyes. True north is relative, I suppose. How did we become coerced in this diabolical plan? I submit that when the epic carving of St. Tolerance was erected in the town hall, we politely applauded and took home a miniature likeness to place on the family mantel. Because we have not purged our country of those who hate us, some of their yeast has gotten into our bread.

The point is that *we* have not been told to sterilize the planet of all who dissent with the Christian beliefs. And so, we continue to try every possible way of making peace and allowing dozens of opportunities for compliance within the world community. The primary assignment is that we not ever be the simpering fools who cower in the corner when the jihadists attempt to commit herem upon all but Islam. Islam *does* know what herem means and they will unflinchingly execute it when the opportunity arises. The threat is real. The data is undeniable. The history is there to see.

Liberal America wants to throw the bi-lateral arm of friendship around known and acid-spitting despots, hand out flowers, apologize for defending ourselves and give 'em another chance to come around. This fellowship will not work. It is un-equal and government officials or aspiring presidential candidates who believe this kind of claptrap cannot be elected or supported. The voting booths are the home bunkers where godly women must hunker down and pull the plug on same-sex marriage, the reduction of homeland security, partial-birth abortions, activist courts, bullying special interest groups, international, kum-bah-yah councils, immoral behaviors by government officials, taxation that parallels the oppression of the Intolerable Acts, government agencies whose sole purpose is the oppression of God-given freedoms, and secular progressives whose days are spent driving around our cities and towns looking for nativity scenes or crosses to fire upon.

WE ARE KNOWN BY THE COMPANY WE KEEP

Now then, as if the command about equal yokes was not enough to create anachronistic commonality, there were more problems. True to the warnings of our Creator, the Israelites who sought fellowship and nuptial bliss with the enemy began to adopt some of the quirky and cute habits of the Canaanites. They began to rationalize little things like the worship of Baal and Ashteroh, or the acceptance of pagan religious practices, false priests, and home décor peppered with the cleverly carved likenesses of those harmless gods. After all, just because you attend a few ceremonies, light a few candles, or rub a few molten tummies; it does not mean you *are* a pagan. It is important to point out that no matter how we feel about the tolerance of such heinous activities, God was not amused. God was offended, angry, and downright hostile. But, mostly, God knew that these practices were not at all harmless.

In fact, the desensitization process is no laughing matter. Ask a prisoner of war if it's a joke. Ask a drug addict if smoking marijuana leads to more drug use. Ask an alcoholic if just one drink is ever enough. Ask a teenager if the time-worn comment, "Everybody does it," still leads to sin. Ask a child if watching violent media even bothers them after a while. And then, ask yourself if playing with fire can be dangerous. Then, just for fun ask a senior citizen about life in the good old USA sixty years ago. Find out what was on T.V. or at the movies or whether or not there was confusion about what the words "is", "adultery", or "marriage" meant. There's a good laugh for you. Only, for those of us who long for a cleaner, clearer country, it is not very funny.

Predictably, opening the barn door or the floodgates or the portal between dimensions (whatever goofy cliché you prefer) for the Israelites led to habits like lying, cheating each other, adultery, and murder. For the Canaanites, these behaviors were part of the collateral damages expected in their "civilization." They were epidemic and the Israelite people were becoming exposed and vulnerable. Again, God's narrow-minded commandments were meant for protection and not cruel restriction. Had the people of God only heeded the commandment to soundly deny themselves from becoming involved in the pagan practices and beliefs of the Canaanites, they would have avoided the coming servitude and oppression.

And, while physical oppression was and is certainly painful, spiritual and moral oppression was and is personal Armageddon. As members of the human family, we can all empathize with those who are caught in the strangle-hold of sins like alcoholism, drug addiction, gambling, pornography, sexual perversion, or the legion menu offered up by the lord host of the netherworld.

So, let us review. The Book of Judges outlines, in its content, a concept known as the sin cycle. In any serious study of the lessons of ancient history through to today's dilemmas, academic conclusions must expose a pattern of greed, depravity, and destruction culminating in the downfall of civilization after civilization. Deborah arrived on the scene at the historical point detailed in chapter four of Judges as the deliverer of the Israelite people. "Here comes the judge" was the harbinger of hope for Israel. That provision by the Lord laid the foundation for deliverance from oppression.

And yes, the people of Israel were being torn to pieces by the lions of greed, depravity, and destruction. Jabin, the king of Canaan had tyrannized the Israelites from the kingdom of Hazor for twenty years. Jabin's power was illustrated by his intimidating fighting force that boasted 900 chariots of iron. It was already known by God's people that they were in dangerous hands, even to their inability to travel the roads without being set upon by marauding Philistines. They had become, literally, prisoners in their own land. Not only were they threatened by Jabin's armies, but were dwelling in and among Hittites, Amorites, Perizzites, Hivites, Moabites, and Jebusites, all members of people groups who both hated them and their God.

Remember, they had been warned and instructed by God. They were to decline any fellowship with the unbelievers of the time. They were to shun the pagan practices. They were even to purge or participate in herem against the inhabitants of the land. What they did was to espouse the opposing behavior. How perplexing! Now, I'm not suggesting that the Israelites should have stepped out, with scimitars blazing, and exterminate the infidel tribes. In fact, that sounds like a terrorist operation to me. But, I am suggesting that the Israelites fell into sinful temptation by, simply, putting their arms around pagan people, practices, and religions.

A BALANCING ACT, AT BEST

In America today, that last sentence would cause such an outcry of unpleasant controversy that I would be touted as a dangerous, radical, right-wing nut! But, that is exactly what I am saying is happening in our great country. We are chanting scary philosophies like: "all is good," "there is good in all," and "condemnation of another philosophy is evil." Now, do not forget that this attitude of omni-acceptance does not extend to radical, right-wing nuts, like me.

Isaiah sounded the selfsame warning cry in this manner:

> *"Woe to those who call evil good, and good evil;*
> *Who put darkness for light, and light for darkness;*
> *Who put bitter for sweet, and sweet for bitter!*
> *Woe to those who are wise in their own eyes,*
> *And prudent in their own sight!"*
>
> ISAIAH 5:20–21

Truly, in our country today, I am asserting that the "people are doing evil in the sight of God and doing what seems right in their own eyes," and are flirting with oppression of a magnitude heretofore unknown to man. If America falls, I pray for the generations to come. It will not be pretty.

This may be the optimal time to take a deep breath, stretch your arms up high over your head, bring them to your side, rock your head side-to-side, and shake yourself awake. If you are ready for some keen observation, just consider some of the following comparisons.

In America today, those who articulate atheism as an acceptable philosophy want to take all of the symbols of God and excise their impact from our public squares, courthouses, government buildings, mottos, pledges, schools, private places of worship, cemeteries, hilltops, T-shirts, banners, hearts, and minds. The bad news is that those of such a hateful ilk are winning the skirmishes and even broadcasting rabid disdain for those who will not acquiesce. We cannot pray in school, at sports events, at graduations, in the courtroom, in our office cubicles, by the flagpole, in the park, or before a national celebration. We are not allowed to use the names of God or Jesus which may result in the social exclusion of persons who do not like Them. It is considered against neo-American protocol to quote the Bible or debate religious philosophies in any public venue.

We are not allowed in our *public schools* to discuss the concept of Creation Science vs. Evolution Theory. Darwinian religion is appropriate to study. Christianity is not. You may wash your feet in the college restrooms, but may not open your Bible in class. Just like the early Believers in the Ancient Middle East, we have been forced to worship deep underground in caverns hidden from the terrorists. And unfortunately, we may be heading for oppression of apocalyptic proportion such as that never before seen. If you believe in the inerrancy of scripture, toddle on over to the Book of Revelation and I'll see you in the "Living, With Anxiety" class. Perhaps, you would rather brainstorm a better solution. I concur.

5

Cycling for the Sake of the Kids

> *"Yet, they would not listen to their judges, but they played the harlot with other gods and bowed down to them. They turned quickly from the way in which their fathers walked, in obeying the commandments of the Lord; they did not do so."*
>
> JUDGES 2:17

THE ISRAELITES IN AND around Ramah and Bethel deliberately compromised their beliefs in the God of Abraham, Isaac, and Jacob, held their tongues, and gave lip service to the idols of the Philistines and the Canaanites in order to maintain fellowship with those who hated them. The result was the excessive burden of oppression, which they tolerated for years until the pain was too great. They cried out to their forgotten Father, and He mercifully commissioned Deborah to deliver them. Can I get a witness?

Okay. We have placed ancient history and our modern day events on a little graph and have illustrated fatally toxic similarity in the realm of marital relationships, religious compromises, and civil tyranny. Surely, that is enough to stir up a shout for relief. I wish it was so. Conversely, it is common to rationalize a decision to ignore these danger signs by branding them "too political for church" or "not what Jesus would do." Anyway, if alternative lifestyles, tranquilized doctrine, and impotence in the public arena are the only parallels, *we are still okay.*

As I seem to have been assigned the dubious honor of being the bearer of more bad news, I would ask you to consider the following. The Israelite people had become un-equally yoked. They had accepted the religious and political lunacy of the inhabitants of Canaan. They had begun to pay homage to false priests and they began to drift epileptically into ritualistic practices. Often these quirky, little pastimes ended in the spilling of innocent blood or debauchery that forever marked the participants. Thanks be to God that we have not fallen to that depth! We are, after all, a civilized country that places inestimable value on human life and respect for others. We don't need saving, yet, because we haven't descended that far. Give me a break. You may want to shut off the Oprah show, close your copy of *The Secret*, and break open an ammonia capsule to clear your head. I have some sobering statistics for you.

SOME STATISTICAL SUPPORT

In 1970, 10.7% of births were illegitimate. By 1990, the figure had jumped to 26.2%. In 1970, 11% of children in America grew up with single mothers. By 1990, that population had doubled to 22%. The violent crime rate in 1970, per 100,000, was 36.42%. In 1990 that figure had skyrocketed to 73%. The teen suicide rate in 1970 was 5.9%. By 1990, 11.3% of our teenagers took their own lives. In 1970, 8.5% of our children lived on welfare. In 1990, children on welfare numbered 11.9%. When I do the math, it looks like bad news had doubled or better in a short, twenty-year period. Three years from 2007 will mark another twenty year period. How do you think we're doing?[1]

Since we are on the subject of children, allow my philosophical wanderings into possible causes for these depressing statistics. Currently, by the time a child is eighteen years old, he or she will witness on television, in movies, on the internet, and in other media, 200,000 acts of violence including 40,000 murders. By the way, between the ages of eight and eighteen, children spend an average of 44.5 hours per week or 6 ½ hours per day in front of computer, television, and game screens. The younger the child, the more vulnerable he/she is. And, surprise! Homicide, suicide, and trauma are the leading causes of death for children, adolescents, and young adults.[2]

While I am pontificating, I may as well opine that the effect of this bludgeoning enclave of violence is greater when the violence is committed by an attractive or charismatic hero(?). Call me stuffy, but where are the supervising parents for 6 ½ hours per day during this powerful train-

---

1. Dr. and Mrs. J. C. Willke, *Why Can't We Love Them Both?* (http://www.abortionfacts.com, last visited 6/29/07).

2. http://www.mediafamily.org/facts/facts_vient.shtml, last visited 6/29/07.

ing time? I mean, the kids have often spent the first 12 hours of their day in a child care center. Is there no possible way that mom or dad could toss them a ball outside for a few minutes?

Now then, those are sad references, aren't they? No one likes to consider that children are being harmed under our watch. But, it is especially disturbing to recognize that the children in question are already survivors of infanticide. I must give credit where credit is due. In Biblical times, infants were torn to pieces on the altars of Baal, in full view of the festival revelers. Today, we have the decency to tear them to pieces in clinics, hospitals, and quiet surgical centers with perky intercom music to underscore the festivities. In 1996, 1.37 million abortions were performed in the good, old USA. That's approximately 3,700 per day. Protestant women obtain about 37.4 % of all abortions, Catholic women account for 31.3%, Jewish women account for 1.3%, women with no religious affiliation obtain 23.7% of all abortions, and 18% of all abortions are performed on women who identify *themselves* to be Born-again or Evangelicals.

And, even more disturbing and less apt to shore up the crumbling foundation set by pro-abortion advocates, their own statistics show that about 93% of these abortions are performed for *social* reasons, with only about 6% being performed because of potential health problems, and about 1% performed because of rape or incest.[3] There goes your best pro-human race argument, down the toilet with the tissue! Talk about throwing out the baby with the crimson water.

If you consider yourself to be a Christian, those facts should be heartbreaking. Of course if you are a pro-choice, pro-murder, pro-human sacrifice American, you're just outraged that I draw the parallel. That same tired, emotional, and utterly non-academic diatribe is tripping off your tongue even now. You are, temples throbbing, screaming something about abortion waste products being just tissue and not baby hands, or that fetuses are not human beings, and I suggest that you might need a simple lesson on the properties of DNA. You may also want to watch a few videos on the horrific practice of partial-birth abortion, or dilatation and extraction, a term coined by Dr. Martin Haskell in 1992 to identify the procedure and make it sound more "medical" and u-h-h "moral". The esteemed Dr. Haskell has performed more than one thousand of these procedures on his own special medical altars. Baal would be proud.

3. http://www.abortionno.org/Resources/fastfacts.html, last visited 6/29/07.

I feel compelled to point out a little island of irony in the midst of this vast, statistical ocean. It seems that to the liberal-leaning mindset, there are *degrees* or *relative levels* of viability, equality, or validity. That makes perfect sense if a measurement is taken based on personal opinion instead of cold, hard facts. But, it is highly questionable to use individual opinion as a technique to insure reliable outcomes or replicable data. I refer you to the striking similarities observed when we juxtapose the historical facts pertaining to the landmark Dred Scott decision of 1857 by the United States Supreme Court and the later Roe v. Wade decision of 1973 that issued forth from the same esteemed body, each of which grappled with the definition of who is or who is not a "legal person" according to the U. S. Constitution.

In both cases, the court was split by a 7-2 vote. Both decisions considered the "non-persons" to be the property of the owner. A black slave was determined to be the property of *its* owner and an un-born child the property of *its* mother (and, I use the term loosely). In 1857, if you owned slaves, you could *choose* to buy, sell, or kill your non-person property. In 1973, if you were pregnant, you were given the right to *choose* to keep or kill your non-person property. Early nineteenth century abolitionists were no longer allowed to impose their morality on slave owners and late twentieth century pro-lifers were then restricted from imposing their morality on pregnant mothers. Slavery and all of its resultant horrors was pronounced legal with the Dred Scott decision, and abortion with all of its resultant horrors was pronounced legal with the Roe v. Wade decision. [4]And, here is the irony. Modern-day liberals are outraged at this treatment of African Americans, but are, feet-planted, four-square in favor of killing babies. What is a reasonable intellectual to do? Oh, yeah. Don't over-think it. Do what seems right in your own eyes, and damned be the history!

As an aside, I should like to give a little round of applause to President George W. Bush for appointing conservatives to the highest court in our land and the subsequent outlawing of the murderous shame of partial-birth abortion. Roe v. Wade, here we come! I would also like to shout out a yea and amen to the prosecutors across our land that charge double murder when a pregnant woman is killed—once for mom, and once for the precious child. P. S. You can't *murder* tissue.

---

4. Dr. and Mrs. J. C. Willke, *Why Can't We Love Them Both?* (http://www.abortion facts.com, last visited 6/29/07).

THE RESULTANT OUTCOMES

So, just to bring us up to speed, consider this. Our children are lonely and depressed. They are, all at once, fascinated and desensitized to the value of human life. They are being nourished by burger joints and cold cereal. They are being nurtured by hand-held games, television, and the internet. By now, they are probably allergic to sunshine, or developing heart disease. We gel their hair into a Mohawk and send them to a public system that is collapsing under the burden of teaching reading, writing, and arithmetic. While there, they experience videos about homosexuality, have open-ended discussions whose faux denouement is the mantra that there is no right answer, are allowed to dress like drunk-driving, promiscuous teen idols, are exposed to the latest fad in education created to replace rules, and phonics, and memorization and junk like that, take their pockets full of money into the candy store or local convenience store to purchase their meal replacement, and get on the daycare bus to await whomever remembers to pick them up there, much later. I would be depressed too. But, what does this all have to do with idol worship or the letting of innocent blood? Come on. You are not that daft!

Catch your breath, if you can, because I am just getting started. In Boston, the health curricula for middle-school students contain instructions on how to use drugs and birth control, wisely. (In middle school, most kids can't even use their lunch money, wisely.) The latest statistics indicate that one in four teen girls has an STD. You know, the kind of thing that can cause sterility, blindness, secondary infections, adhesions, lifelong illness, and even end your life. Liberal thinkers propose that the solution is what they glibly call "condom education." Apparently, that hasn't stopped the raging diseases. In their haste to avoid the conception of life, their tactic has been unable to quell death. Kindergarten students across the nation are exposed to films like "It's Elementary", a dandy, little movie promoting alternative lifestyles, tolerance, and disdain for their old-fashioned parents.

The ACLU is rabidly defending the first amendment rights of the likes of NAMbLA (small b for the little boys, big M for the big perverts) to advertise their perversions on the internet, complete with suggestive pictures and the proposal that the children are consenting partners in this filth. The ACLU is up-front and center in the lawsuits brought by Michael Newdow of the great state of California, as he prances into the

Ninth Circuit Court of appeals and a federal court in Sacramento in an effort to remove any mention of God from the pledge. His next move? He would like to remove the words, "In God We Trust" from our currency. Little, baby Jesus bugs him, too, and Merry Christmas, and crosses, and YOU. Mr. Newdow is no surprise an atheist. He maintains that there is no God. He should not be offended when God announces that there is no Michael Newdow.

While we are on the subject of citizens against God, take a look at a rabid organization responsible for deadly and destructive civil disobedience in the name of preserving and protecting the environment. I'm talking about ELF, or the Earth Liberation Front, who travel this fair land setting fire to SUV dealerships, ski resorts, luxury homes, water bottling plants, and...? These eco-terrorists are the self-imposed protectors of the planet earth and do not care which of you gets in their way on the crusade. You see, in their opinion, you are the problem. And so, just like little babies who get in the way of their mommy's social calendar, earth-rapers (their term) have got to go. If they kill or endanger a few humans on the way, it's no big whoop.

The group lacks central government, so it is comprised of many wandering bands of Robin Hood-like characters, which makes them hard to catch and even harder to interview on Fox news. But, then again, once all the babies are dead, the ELFs must exterminate the full-grown humans in order to make room for the plants, and trees, and animals, and Peter Singer, the patron saint of all who have carved idols that pay homage to nature and the animals.

The point is that human life and the sure knowledge that the God who created all of this can certainly take care of it is the very kindling from whence their fires originate. They want to be god, not because they think they can do better, really. They just don't like the real One. How does any of this relate to our subject matter? Well... the people are doing what seems right in their own eyes, deifying everything *but* God, killing the innocent, participating in criminal activity, and (as in Peter Singer's case) advocating sodomy, the killing of disabled children and fetuses (his word), and that animals must exist with humans in a community of equals. Take home a nice, little statue of your favorite phenomenon of nature and light up a candle in its name. Or, better yet, light up the neighbor's house. Deliver us, oh Lord. We are undone!

Hey, Peter! Have you heard this one?

> *"Professing to be wise, they became fools and changed the glory of the incorruptible God into an image made like corruptible man—and birds and four-footed animals and creeping things. Therefore God also gave them up to uncleanness, in the lusts of their hearts, to dishonor their bodies among themselves, who exchanged the truth of God for the lie and worshipped and served the creature rather than the Creator, who is blessed forever. Amen!"*
>
> Romans 1:22–25

6

Sin Squared

> *"The heart is deceitful above all things, and desperately wicked; Who can know it?"*
>
> JEREMIAH 17:9

BY NATURE OF REVIEW, in the days of Deborah and Barak, the Israelite people had defied the counsel of God and had inter-married with the pagan population. They were either condoning or participating in the worship of false idols and pagan gods. God's children had become proficient at lying, rationalizing, and blaming. They were involved in religious rituals that included paying bloody homage to graven images, the practice of sexual perversions, sodomy and human sacrifice, and ritualistic revelries, often under the influence of drugs, alcohol, and demonic inhabitations.

The fourth chapter of Judges says it this way:

> *"When Ehud was dead, the children of Israel again did evil in the sight of the Lord. So, the Lord sold them into the hand of Jabin, king of Canaan, . . ."*
>
> JUDGES 4:1–2

What I am trying to illustrate here is that the phrase; ". . . did evil in the sight of the Lord . . ." encompassed then and encompasses now the same practices and unconscionable behaviors that we have already discussed. What we must focus on, now, is the very next phrase from that scripture reference. It warns; "So, the Lord sold them into the hand of Jabin, the king of Canaan . . ."

So, love you, but . . . the people were delivered up to the oppressors . . . How can we possibly draw any comparison of life in America today to the oppression of the Israelites by the Canaanites? Well, let's see.

THE PATH TO OPPRESSION

I grew up in the 50s. The nuclear family i.e. a social unit comprised of father, mother, and children, was the only acceptable lifestyle. Alternative lifestyles were understood to be those whose life's decisions determined whether they lived in a house, a trailer, the desert, the mountains, on a farm, or in the city. I know this is sounding like a Dr. Seuss book, but that's how it was. We certainly were *not* the "Father Knows Best" perfect units without dysfunctions or problems. But, we aspired to be. Now, I know that many of you, professional and lay person alike, will suggest that those beginnings are what spawned a nation of pill-popping, booze-drinking, and suicide-committing adults. But, you are the un-repentant, angry cynics among us. That's not my point, anyway. My point is that families were important. Marriage was considered sacred, an institution to be entered with commitment and absent of an early exit strategy.

In the 50s, we thought everyone with any sense, believed in God. Those few on the outer fringe of propriety, who did not, were relegated to the halls of liberal education or vomiting their vitriol into underground newspapers. We were expected to respect and honor our elders, believed that America *was* the land of the free and the home of the brave. My mom baked cupcakes for my school bake sale. My dad went to work every day and came home at night, on time. We learned reading, writing, and arithmetic at school. Health education was limited to nutrition, hygiene, and physical exercise. A few of our fellow students got pregnant or contracted social diseases, but I felt bad for them. Almost all of the basic social ills existed: disease, crime, wars, abuse, death, abortion, abandonment, starvation, racism, selfishness, greed, yata, yata, yata.

As a young, liberal-leaning adult, I thought our hope was in anti-establishment protest, peace and flower-power, and Bobby Kennedy. In my tempestuous teens and early twenties, I was furious about racism, archaic social rules, and the unequal distribution of wealth, guns, and opportunity. The tumultuous 60's brought enlightenment and true freedom. If it feels good, do it. That was the battle cry. What really had begun many years earlier, outside of my middle-America cocoon, was now a voraciously growing butterfly. The people were doing what was right in their own eyes, as is the nature of man. And, even though a systematic study of how we got here would be really great reading, it is not my purpose. I am suggesting that we are oppressed in America, and I wanted to lead us, philosophically, from the frying pan and into the fire.

Liberal thinking brought us to the twenty-first century with a national government that barely resembles the one "conceived in liberty and dedicated to the proposition that all men are created equal," to one that maintains a civil system wherein citizens are now guilty until proven innocent. In our businesses, we are required to follow regulation after insipid regulation in an atmosphere of oppressive taxation without even the slightest representation. We rationalize the local threat that our property can be seized in the name of eminent domain and the betterment of the community, and possess a gulag-mentality wherein genocide and euthanasia are cocktail party conversation.

We selfishly support the assertion that children should neither be seen nor heard but rather placed in government-regulated daycares while we pursue our careers. Our government and union-run schools are training grounds for social deviancy and curricula agendas that are, at best, intellectually dishonest, and, at worst, brainwashing. Fathers are leaving their children and mothers are leaving their children to go and "find themselves." Sadly, the streets of our cities are battle fields where children must run the gauntlet, hourly, avoiding drugs, perversions, and bullets. The graphic portrayal of violence in the media, video games, and children's literature is poisoning our kids, slowly and certainly.

Our national heroes commit adultery in the oval office. While homosexuality and pedophilia are protected by the first amendment, religion is discouraged, and Bibles cannot be brought into public settings where prayer is also prohibited.

The police are beating the life out of detainees way before their Miranda rights are read, airplane rides are a criminal investigation experience, babies are being given illegal drugs by their caregivers, animals are being tortured in the name of sport, and husbands are drowning, strangling, blasting, and knifing their pregnant wives and dumping their bodies in the wilderness or the lake. Our children are being executed in the libraries of their schools by their fellow students, and college girls/babies/little girls and boys/teens are being snatched, raped, and murdered by socio-paths, dismembered, and buried alive.

The Israelites were becoming liars, murderers, and adulterers, and participating in pagan rituals. What of us?

Even though I am keenly aware that the last few comments may be viewed as skewed thinking by secular progressive standards, the facts are, certainly, undeniable. And, please, do not think that I am un-aware of the supernaturally wonderful things that happen in our country, today. I am not a gloom and doom reactionary, but lean more toward being a realist and, therefore, a problem solver. Of course, we must agree on the nature of the problem before any amelioration can succeed. And, I am sure that around 1200 B.C., the Israelites wrestled with an even-handed assessment of their current situation. *Not.*

WHAT THE ISRAELITES KNEW THAT WE DON'T

The Israelites were living under the governance of terrorists who were marauding after them in the streets and raping them in their towns. God's people were un-equally yoked in marriage, in business, in social inter-actions, in religious practices, and in their position with the government. The Canaanites were not concerned about the liberty and equality of the followers of the Old Testament teachings and traditions. In fact, those teachings and traditions were not allowed in the public square or even in the privacy of their homes.

In other words, placing a scroll of the Ten Commandments next to a nice carving of Ashteroh or upon a sweet, little depiction of the altar of Baal was, often, a death sentence. The worship of Yahweh was conducted deep underground or under great threat to life and limb. Basically, they were surrounded. The Philistines inhabited the outer areas of their cities, as well as the sea coasts. The Canaanites, Hivites, Perizzites, Amorites, Moabites, etc, etc. surrounded them on the inland, upland, and down land sides.

And so, in order to keep peace and be as un-molested as possible, the people of God attempted to live morally, absent of any reference to the God of Abraham, Isaac, and Jacob. Deborah, I am sure, suffered the thankless job of reminding the Israelites where they had gone wrong and was, most probably, considered to be the epitome of intolerance and stubborn allegiance to God. Still, the Israelites had then, as they do now, a certain reverence for their traditions and laws. And, they had the presence of mind to repent and call out to the Lord for deliverance.

Today, in our churches and in our civil duties, we are trying to perform the selfsame balancing act. We want morality and peace. We just shot ourselves in the foot by allowing the removal of the only cogent foundation *for* that morality from our arsenal. Now, we have a raging battle to fight whose outcome will determine the very existence of our nation's blessing, and we stammer some ridiculous statement like; "As a nation, we, first and foremost, stand for tolerance and compromise." In 1776, that would have been cause for vigorous debate, ending in fisticuffs.

If we are all still reasoning together, allow me to elaborate on the title of this chapter. It has been said that if God continues to exercise patience with the behaviors of the peoples of the world today, He must really apologize to Sodom and Gomorrah. Now, if you are a left-leaning type, that comment bugs you exponentially. You find that statement to be loony-bin worthy. (I'm sorry. Loony bin may be politically incorrect. Change that to religious ranting. It's okay to demean that people group.)

Still, the liberal left continues to shout from the housetops about tolerance, equality, don't ask, don't tell, (unless you carry a concealed weapon, and then you must declare), personal rights, and their abhorrence of value judgments. And, here I am, concluding that we live in a country that is rapidly becoming a steaming cesspool and that something monumental must be done to deliver us. Unfortunately, Deborah will not be coming, today. I do think, however, that she may be watching.

It is altogether significant that we cross reference this concept to the historical citings in the Book of Judges. With the passage of time and the Divine appointment of each judge deliverer, we observe a descending cycle. Each new generation under a new deliverer sinned "more than their fathers." Additionally, each new judge was respected and supported less than the one previous until the time of the last deliverer, Samson, who was bound by the people he had come to save and turned over to the enemy. That kind of gratitude just stimulates intense emotion, don't you think?

Additionally, it is truly fitting that the Biblical book of Joshua, preceding Judges, ends with a farewell address from its namesake. We would be foolish to believe that the promise of Abraham unfolded like a set of clean, crisp sheets, was smoothed out, and lay across God's people in peaceful slumber. Oh, they were asleep, alright. It's just that someone started tossing and turning and "kicking against the goads", and the covers got all screwed up. We know this because in Joshua's farewell he warned;

> "Therefore, take careful heed to yourselves that you love the Lord your God. Or else, if indeed you do go back, and cling to the remnant of these nations—these that remain among

> *you—and make marriages with them, and go in to them and they to you, know for certain that the Lord your God will no longer drive out these nations from before you. But they shall be snares and traps to you, and scourges on your sides and thorns in your eyes, until you perish from this good land which the Lord your God has given you."*
>
> JOSHUA 23:11–13

And then, we begin the first chapter of the account of the Israelite people in the book of Judges as the tribes continue the process of challenging and routing out the Canaanites. In chapter two the death of Joshua is recounted followed by these words:

> *"Then the children of Israel did evil in the sight of the Lord and served the Baals; and they forsook the Lord God of their fathers, who had brought them out of the land of Egypt; and they followed other gods from among the gods of the people who were all around them, and they bowed down to them; and they provoked the Lord to anger. They forsook the Lord and served Baal and the Ashtoreths."*
>
> JUDGES 2:11–13

Someone started screwing up the blankets. And, from the arrival of Othniel until the demise of Samson, really nifty gods of all ilks tempted the people to leave their first love and tumble down the slippery slope with ever-increasing speed and debauchery.

Historical accounts of the ancient peoples illustrate the decline of all that was decent and righteous into the most heinous and reprehensible sin imaginable. The people would have done well to heed a warning similar to the teachings in Proverbs 1:31: *"Therefore, they shall eat the fruit of their own way, and be filled to the full with their own fancies."* Or, as my father used to paraphrase: "You're gonna' reap what you sow." Who knew any of this stuff would have real meaning in the twenty-first century? Oh, yeah—God.

You see, without God, we are standing on a dual foundation—the ever-shifting sand of public policy and opinion and our false confidence in power-hungry tyrants. We *are* oppressed, and it is time to cry out for deliverance. Barak needed the urging, and ultimately, the presence of Deborah on the battlefield. Women of faith in America today are no less potent than was she. We can advise, urge, and even force change. It is just so vital that we do it! If we do not stand in that gap, in a few more years, I will be afraid to look at the outcome. Guess what? We are not inhabitants of the Promised Land. God has no covenant with America, short of this one:

> *"If My people, who are called by My name will humble themselves, and pray and seek My face, and turn from their wicked ways, then I will hear from heaven, and will forgive their sin and heal their land."*
>
> 2 Chronicles 7:14

7

The Enemy Is Us

> *"But each one is tempted when he is drawn away by his own desires and enticed. Then, when desire has conceived, it gives birth to sin; and sin when it is full-grown, brings forth death."*
>
> JAMES 1:14–15

NOT TOO LONG AGO, I had the occasion to visit with a friend who was suffering from the AIDS virus. That this was a horrific experience for him was a given. I was humbled, clumsy, and inadequate at his bedside. Even though it had been my questionably esteemed honor to be the first person with whom he had shared the nightmare of his diagnosis, I was devastated and unprepared. This young man was one of the brightest and most creative minds I had ever known. He was talented, assured, and would have easily been voted the "most likely to . . ." But, that was not to be his end. I awkwardly attempted to give him the message of forgiveness and salvation offered to us by our Savior. He was filled with such anger, grief, and regret, that he soundly routed me out for what he considered to be my presumptuous, holier-than-thou hate rhetoric and sent me away. He died with other more tolerant folks holding his hand. Hah! That showed me!

Because of that experience, I know that the message of this book is equally unpalatable to those who have a philosophical bone to pick with the religious right. And, I suppose I learned nothing from that earlier shunning. Even though my approach and advice were given with a fear and trembling I had not known before, in a society of inclusion worship, I was a pariah. At least, that is what we might hear pummeling us from the all-inclusive airways of today. Never mind that I truly loved and mourn the loss of that friend. Never mind that I truly believe that the definitive work concerning the lessons of life is the Bible. And, never mind that I did not make the rules. God did.

You see, it was, likely, an act of bravado that caused the Prophetess Deborah to approach Barak and remind him that there were some instructions that he seemed to be ignoring. Remember, Deborah was intelligent and wise and well informed on the issues of the day. You can bet that she also knew her place.

Oh boy. I'm sure I just registered red alert on the female talk show host hit list. And even though I am not a billionaire with flamboyant hair, someone out there would love to get their ad hominem argument around my neck—you know, no substance, just vitriol. Nevertheless, good historians do not present the events of the past with a contemporary spin. Deborah was a judge. She was not a battle commander. And, she was not in the habit of imposing her tactical strategy suggestions on Barak.

WHERE WE ARE GOING WRONG

Today's Congress could take a lesson from Deborah and stay out of the face-to-face deliberations of war. I could be wrong, of course, if our Speaker of the House has experienced a visitation of Biblical proportion and been commanded to deliver an ultimatum to the Generals in charge of the boots on the ground in Iraq. It would seem to be incongruent for the current majority party to, suddenly, look to God for guidance. After all, such a monolithic assent to intolerant, Judeo-Christian ethics would certainly herald the collapse of their liberal sleight of hand. So, if my assumptions are correct and God has not spoken to the Congressional majority party leaders, there are some serious domestic problems that need their attention, like the simplification of our tax system, or the re-vamping of social security, or our dependence on foreign oil, or the existence of terrorist sleeper cells in our quiet suburbs, to name a very few.

Deborah did not inject herself into military decisions. She saw disobedience in Barak and, rightfully, according to promptings from God, compelled him to fight the good fight. I hate to be such a downer, but Deborah did not suggest that Barak retreat, establish benchmarks, or start a diplomatic dog-and-pony show in a country where a twelve-year-old boy is praised for gleefully sawing a man's head off as several of his "elders" hold the victim down. She told him that God expected him to win the battle so that the Israelite people could be safe in the land. Since Barak was unwilling to go it alone, Deborah went forward into battle with him, all the while knowing that God had gone before and that Barak would forever be beholden to a woman for the victory.

That would not play well on "The View" because Deborah told the general to fight and destroy the enemy. War-mongering (their word) women of integrity (mine) don't make the director's cut. War-undermining (their tactic) bitter women's libbers (my unpopular take) do. Sadly for them, their political triage model is disorganized. Much more could be gained for the liberal platform if they played up the end of the story, touting the creativity and bravery of Jael, a woman. But, wait, Jael was on the side of the Believers and that kind of an intolerant traitor could never be a NOW poster girl. Please excuse my mistake.

We have already visited some of the philosophical, political, and contemporarily topical grindage (stuff to chew on) that exposes similarities of life in America today with the experiences of the Israelites in and around 1200 B.C. Of course, the Herculean task of cataloging *every* occurrence of disobedience to God's Word in our country would not only be daunting, but left unread by anyone who has relegated tomes like, "Crime and Punishment" or "War and Peace" to their never-read pile.

So, now I want to get up close and personal. I'm going to nit-pick. It is my time to expound on the rationalizations du'jour as I see it in our country and in our Christian brothers and sisters. Rest assured, I have been roundly criticized and shunned for these opinions. Jesus warned me. His true disciples are not welcome in the world. If your liberal leanings, outright leftist DNA, or seeker-friendly mindset, settle on your life like a much-needed root canal does on a tooth, STOP right now and hate me for the preceding information. Please put this book next to "War and Peace" and be gone!

AN IDOL IS AN IDOL IS AN IDOL

Still here? Welcome to Idols 101. There will not be a syllabus for this class. You will be creating your own as we go. Your pre-requisite course must have included Applied Mathematics so that the concept of "squaring" a number may be easily transferred to the concept of "squaring" your sin. In the good old days, squaring with someone meant making it right. In math class, squaring something means making it huge. I want to show you how fast yeast can permeate our loaves.

Let's begin with a definition. The "Random House College Dictionary" defines an idol as 1) an image, as a statue or other material object, *worshipped* as a deity, or 3) any person or thing, *devotedly or excessively admired*. (The emphases are mine.)

Since we have already explored the signs of terminal disease in our society, further comment is unnecessary. As Christians, we recognize the fireworks display of major sin before our eyes. But, as in most cases of serious disease, we often ignore those symptoms leading up to the debilitating event. My purpose in this section of the book is to explore the advent of the symptoms that brought us to the destructive events of the day. Please understand that we did not get to this awful point overnight.

The Israelites in Deborah's day began their rapid descent into hell by first minimizing the importance of the *whole* of God's commands. So first, we must agree that America is in hell. If you still think we are okay, step aside. I need heroines who will take this call to arms seriously. Remember that the Israelites were *oppressed*. They were miserable, suffering, being terrorized, raped, and killed. You must believe that, in America today, we are in the same situation. So, if you think our government is okay, our schools are okay, our kids are okay, our streets are safe, our liberty and freedom are inviolate, our personal health and safety are respected, or that the beliefs upon which this country were founded are still thriving, go and rub the tummy of your favorite possession. You are not ready to cry out to a Holy God for deliverance. Have a nice day.

I should now be speaking to the warriors. Come, let us reason together.

OUR HISTORY AS A GUIDE

With the winding down of World War II, Americans began the task of building a stronger and safer America. We were experiencing many domestic challenges. Our international challenges were also expanding and becoming more inclusive while our citizens were becoming less discerning. An example of this might be the willingness of our government to begin trading and participating in diplomacy with the "whole world." The United Nations was established in June of 1945, largely, by the victors of the Second World War. The publicly stated paramount goal was to avoid the horror of future world wars. Again, a capable mathematician may wonder from whence all of the resultant agencies connected with today's United Nations sprang.

Domestically, we were struggling with rebuilding our financial and social systems. And, to add to the challenge, soldiers were coming home to their anxious wives and families, with the resultant outcome of an unprecedented birthrate explosion. America was not only "New Dealing" with a war-torn citizenry, but an ever burgeoning census. Since FDR had opened one of those trick cans of peanuts filled with spring-loaded worms in 1933, more conservative folks had begun the process of buffering the expanding damages done by social programs that were growing like bacteria, and by 1943 had petitioned the Supreme Court about the constitutionality of these exclusive programs. The Supreme Court sided with the Constitution. That is how it used to be.

We struggled through the rest of the 1940s, entered the 1950s and the Cold War with dreams of owning our own homes, raising our incomes and our families, building our cities and infrastructures, designing our bomb shelters, and worshipping according to our own consciences on the Lord's Day. The 1960s intruded into our most sanctified places with cries of free love, peace, and down with the establishment. We lifted one eyelid out of the sand, where our heads had been juxtaposed, and blamed drugs, sex, and rock-and-roll. With the 70s, 80s, 90s, and on to the turn of the twenty-first Century, came a growing sense of concern and, for many of us, figuratively seated between the palms, an overwhelming nausea. America was nursing the worst yeast infection in the history of the world.

Probably you are very indignant right now. How dare I conclude that America is worse than, say, the Roman Empire with their dubious heroes like Nero and Caligula? Do I mean that we even come close to the horrors of Nazi Germany? Am I suggesting that the streets of our country even somewhat parallel the killing fields of Saddam Hussein's Iraq? Who do I think I am?

Well—when we began this study, I proclaimed that America was in trouble and needed a deliverer akin to Judge Deborah, circa 1200 B.C. I am hoping to convince you to agree with my premise by presenting you with today's definition of "un-equally yoked." If you are sticking with me, don't look back, the secular progressives are gaining on you like the Urak'ai chasing the Fellowship of the Ring. Just keep your focus on God and run with all your might.

AN EXERCISE IN SELF-EVALUATION

To what do you pay homage? I own a childcare and private school business. I watch the comings and goings of lots of people every day. I serve the rich, the struggling, and the median income recipients. My clients are the bold, beautiful, and the challenged who are seeking every day for some sort of peace and prosperity. Ours is a Christian Center, so we are a little cloistered, I know. Nevertheless, this is my thirty-seventh year in the field, and I have seen it all. Here is what I know.

We have children who are left in our school for more than ten hours a day on a regular basis. Mothers and fathers are working longer and longer, and seeking relief from child-rearing, more and more. We see this in the government school system, as parents attend fewer and fewer parent-teacher conferences, express irritation when called to school during the day, and tend not to know who is teaching or what is being taught to their child. Add to that the increasing incidence of teachers who cannot even remember or differentiate between their students because the commitment and personal relationship inherent in the call to teach is no longer present nor desired and you have opened a Pandora's box. Even the people of God are content to allow possibly amoral and marginally involved personnel to nurture, educate, and raise their kids.

After daycare, their kids are treated to a nourishing children's meal at the local drive-up window. They go home to an evening of video games or R-rated movies, and who-knows-how-it's-rated television. They have no set schedule or bedtime. Often, they are bathed intermittently, and almost never nightly. They mimic the filthy language that they hear, (imagine that?) laugh at the expense of others, aggressively acquire whatever they want, and disrespect the commands of their adults. I do not have to tell you how those early experiences play themselves out in the teen-aged and young adult years. Because our Center is Christian, our children and families can expect that we *will* "train up the children in the way they should go." Most are not so lucky.

Childhood obesity and diabetes are on a scary rise. Our cities are peppered with youth treatment centers, youth incarceration programs, and violence in the streets that is taking the lives of tomorrow's hope. Single-parent families are prevalent. Alternative families and alternative lifestyles are wreaking havoc on delicate psyches and feelings of emotional well-being and safety. Committed marriages are waning as divorce becomes just "no big deal." Millions of kids go home to empty houses, every day. Moms are leaving their families, dads are leaving their families, and kids are leaving their families. Parents are impotent in their responsibilities, and government agencies are taking the helm. The secular progressive agenda is bombarding us from all of life's venues.

Who can spot the idol? Is it the career idol, the money idol, the personal space idol, the personal choice idol, the laziness idol, the appearances idol, the physical beauty idol, the fame idol, the hobby idol, the union idol, the personal peace and fulfillment idol, the ego, the id, the self-esteem idol? Oh, deliver us, Lord, for we are undone! God commands:

> *"Wives, submit to your own husbands, as to the Lord."*
>
> EPHESIANS 5:22

> *"Husbands love your wives*
> *just as Christ also loved the church..."*
>
> EPHESIANS 5:25A

> *"Children, obey your parents in the Lord, for this is right."*
>
> EPHESIANS 6:1

Lest I avoid offending everyone, it is imperative that I continue to lift up a few more examples.

I am often perplexed by our parents who remove their children from the Christian school in their middle school and high school years. While I am sure that those parents would have highly developed explanations for the move, it just comes back to one issue. Their kids desire the programs, socialization, and opportunities afforded them by the government systems.

One family wanted their son to be a football star, and truly believed that he would rise to the NFL only by beginning grape-vine exercises in the seventh grade. Another family expressed their belief that their thirteen-year old daughter could be "salt and light" to her friends at the local middle school. She was already wearing low-riders, globs of make-up, and belly shirts on the weekends. Another family wanted their son to have a more flexible class schedule, allowing for more variety of curricula.

I could go on for pages about the families that chose four-wheelers, camping trailers, motorboats, bigger houses, new cars, or big-screen TV's over the expense of private school. That is just unconscionable. Don't go there with me. I have given up having my own cars, houses, and meals in order to serve a needy family or under-funded student many, many times and provide what education I could.

In the category of long-story-short, the rising football star, dropped out of school and is nowhere to be seen on the NFL radar. The up-and-coming ingénue turned to the dark side, but, grace of God, her parents woke up and put her back into a Christian school. She leaves for Christian college this year. Praise God, alone! Mr. Flexible Schedule cannot hold a job or choose a career to save his life, today. Unfortunately, he has his own family that struggles every day to keep the future stable.

I submit that sports can be an idol, friendships can be an idol, endless variety and change can be an idol, possessions can most certainly be an idol. But to spare you the procession of sappy stories, just imagine your own scenarios attached to an obsessive love of movies, money, systems, unions, work, school, church, career, beauty, youth, power, fame, hobbies, intellectual prowess, or heroes. The list is pitifully incomplete, but you could provide your own thoughts if you are very brave. If not, just refer to this warning: "The people were doing what seemed right in their own eyes." Where is a spiritual optometrist when we need one?

I know that most of us are comfortably nestled down in our unholy relationships. I know that our carefully carved belongings seem innocuous. And, I know that a little yeast can be a wonderful thing when applied to the perfect loaf. However, I also know that de-sensitization is insidious business. In the beginning, sin is so veiled in neutral skin that we settle down like worms in a pan of cool water, awaiting the boil, not even noticing the rise in temperature. Having been involved in a de-humanizing and abusive relationship in my youth, I can testify that the weight of its destruction was only appreciated when it was over. I stood back from the fire and, finally, saw that the list of incendiary scars was legion.

I have not even drawn allusion to those capital subjects so quickly on our collective tongues during these types of exchanges. I am referring to our disdain for the propagation of drug abuse, alcohol abuse, sexual abuse, the evils of pornography or gambling, the chipping away of our foundations by alternative lifestyles, infanticide to harvest immortality, and the fleecing of Americans by narcissistic and socio-pathetic purveyors of physical beauty, great wealth, fame, or personal power. We all know those guys are evil. We talk about them over donuts and Starbucks mocchiato but few of us react in such a way as to expunge them from our midst. Truly, we are not talking about you, here.

And so, perhaps, your idols are in storage, hopefully, never to return. I pray that for you. Just remember that we are exploring the state of our union, i.e. the United States of America. How is our country doing, and could you do more to effect a change? As women of faith, I submit that we can. Soon, I will explain a few possible techniques. Until then, this discussion serves to point out the festering infection, not yet uncomfortable enough to activate the seeking of a cure. But, like so many fatal diseases, the early symptoms may be purposefully and arrogantly ignored, usually with dire result.

> *"And even as they did not like to retain God in their knowledge, God gave them over to a debased mind, to do those things which are not fitting; being filled with all unrighteousness, sexual immorality, wickedness, covetousness, maliciousness; full of envy, murder, strife, deceit, evil-mindedness; they are whisperers, backbiters, haters of God, violent, proud, boasters, inventors of evil things, disobedient to parents, undiscerning, untrustworthy, unloving, unforgiving, unmerciful; who, knowing the righteous judgment of God, that those who practice such things are deserving of death, not only do the same but also approve of those who practice them."*
>
> Romans 1:28–32

THE NEEDS OF THE MANY OUTWEIGH THE NEEDS OF THE ONE

Often, as comfort and peace seeking adults, we turn to sureness and solid information to salve our ills. It is common to add all of our lifelong columns up and reach a sum that is utilitarian for our chosen situation. What I *mean* is: Who or what is your final authority? Upon what basis do you resolve data and make decisive claims? In other words, how do you deliberate choices? At its core, what do you believe and why?

I imagine that many of you have never been asked or asked yourselves those questions. Frighteningly, most of us proceed on what *just feels right*.

If that statement refers to you, the looming specter of oppression is just over your shoulder. That is the stuff of enslavement to counterfeit beliefs and systems. Get ready to dive into extra-Biblical books, extra-sensory experiences, extra-ordinary activities, and an extra-oppressive existence. You might want to review the proceeding information on personal idols.

I pose these questions to stimulate research into your views of authority and your source, thereof. Because, no matter what area of cognitive understanding we propose, everyone has that final author of their beliefs. As small children, our parents or extended family members shaped not only our behaviors but our opinions. Theoretically, during those formative years, those are the champions who protect and provide. However, it does not take long before the human spirit and our inherited nature causes us to react like pearls nudging sand particles away.

In early adolescence, we question all things, most especially authority. Most, having not been taught the science of logic, fly into all sorts of emotional flailing against the status quo. The true academic would assent to the logical argument that our American concept of individual freedom is a part of that paradigm. But, also, we must conclude that the environment into which one is birthed has some effect.

As we go, hurtling out into adult life, these basic beliefs cling to us. And, unless, we are forced by a life's stressor or invited by a formative experience to change, we remain the same. Therefore, if your family's beliefs were Catholic, Protestant, Muslim, Wiccan, Mormon, pro-choice, pro-life, Republican, Democrat, Libertarian, racist, hippy, free economist, socialist, isolationist, hawk or dove, your views most often parallel those. If your people were poor, wealthy, southern, northern, educated, alienated, land owners, land workers, teachers, doctors, franchise owners, or homeless, the chances are good that your life is a reflection of that base. That is, of course, if those foundational tenets espoused to you were never questioned *by* you.

If the proceeding paragraph sounds like kindling for an excuse, you don't get me. I am not a social scientist, by trade, or a therapist, by certification. I am a daughter of the Most High God who sees trouble brewing between and amongst the palms. If you have not questioned your beliefs since you were mouthing strained peas, in some ways, you are still there. I think your mom and pop were heroes, too, especially if they stayed together and kept your home sacrosanct. But, unless your family had at its firmest foundation, the irrefutable and inerrant truths contained in the

Word of God, The Bible, it is wake up time. There just aren't any counterfeit truths that will withstand the tests of all ilks like the original truth, The Bible.

I am reminded of the saying; "If it is true, it is probably not new. And, if it is new, it is probably not true." Yeah. Yeah. I am aware that many discoveries through the ages were unknown and unavailable at differing times during the development of the world of today. Certainly, much has been given to us for our blessing. That just means that, like purchasing clothing at a second-hand store, those items are new to us and eternally true to Creator God.

Allow me to expose just a few of the many final authorities that may or may not be guiding your life. We may conduct ourselves with unwavering commitment to a pastor or religious leader, a government, a teacher or professor, a philosopher or musician, science or academics, the media, a performer, a scholar, a hero, a therapist, a medical doctor, family, friends, or the ever-popular feelings, emotions, and impressions already targeted in our discussion.

Now, I know that we are familiar with the dangers in this ideology. Men will fail, make mistakes, be lured by sin, give bad advice, and formulate emerging and evolving ideations. Exhibits of this inherent type of danger might include the questionable careers of Jim Jones, Adolph Hitler, Karl Marx, Richard Nixon, the executives of Enron, or Napoleon at Waterloo. Additionally marketed follies might point to the assurance by our government that down-winders were not going to be harmed by underground testing, the industry hype that asbestos was a fine insulation, the approval by the FDA of drugs or therapies that prove to be dangerous or even deadly, etc., etc., etc.

Truly, if you had risked your entire fortune on a horse at Hyalea, you would, at least, have been playing odds and knowingly gambled your future. But, if you are blindly following a mutable and imperfect man or his system, review quickly the formulative criteria that put you at risk in the first place.

Often, I am taken to task by an unbeliever for my intolerance. Hah! Isn't that funny? Oh. I forgot. If you were publicly educated, you most likely never took a formal logic class. You see, the joke is that *he* is being intolerant of my intolerance! These kinds of Oreo cookie arguments are treated with contempt by liberal leftists. Unfortunately, the truth of the matter is that my chocolate cookie and your chocolate cookie are held parallel by the creamy truth within. Without that cohesive substance, each of us would just be careening across the galaxy looking for our place. (Please, don't make the obvious Milky Way joke. It is beneath you.)

I stand on the firm and sure knowledge that the Bible is inerrant and would be happy to discuss your differing opinion as long as you have the facts and not just the wrath. Even if just the simple and primary requirements of The Ten Commandments were used as the parameter for right and wrong, each of the aforementioned people and circumstances would prove to be in opposition to those basic rules. Historically, archeologically, linguistically, anthropomorphically, mathematically, and scientifically, The Bible continues to be a proven source of truth. If that sounds intolerant, so be it. *Prove* me wrong and I will stand down.

Conversely, if I am right, women of faith everywhere must begin to re-shape and prod our leaders in to battle. Not one more infant should die. Not one more family should starve. Not one more sacred institution should fall. Not one more criminal should go free. Not one more lie should be told. Not one more evil dictator should be tolerated. Not one more drug dealer or terrorist should be allowed to cross our borders. Not one more political smear campaign should be allowed to cloud the real issues. Not one more hateful and traitorous citizen should be afforded the benefits of our free speech. Not one more liberal judge or court should be retained who legislates from the bench. And, not one more of our precious freedoms bought for us by the blood, sweat, and tears of our founding fathers, our soldiers, and our citizens should be sacrificed. Please, heed the warning:

> *"But know this, that in the last days perilous times will come: For men will be lovers of themselves, lovers of money, boasters, proud, blasphemers, disobedient to parents, unthankful, unholy, unloving, unforgiving, slanderers, without self-control, brutal, despisers of good, traitors, headstrong, haughty, lovers of pleasure, rather than lovers of God, having a form of godliness, but denying its power. And from such people turn away! For of this sort are those that creep into households and make captives of gullible women loaded down with sins, led away by various lusts, always learning and never able to come to the knowledge of the truth."*
>
> 2 Timothy 3:1–7

8

Hope Revisited

*"Now faith is the substance of things hoped for,
the evidence of things not seen."*

HEBREWS 11:1

NOW THEN, ALL OF us have, no doubt, experienced a visit either as a visi*tor* or the reciprocal visi*ted*. Most likely, each of us also has personal recollection of visi*ting* and its polar opposite, *going away*. We like all of these things. We often especially appreciate the going away part when our visitors have perhaps overstayed their ability to be tolerable. But, the term *re*-visited presupposes that the phenomenon has occurred before. And, in fact, that is our beginning reference point now as we hearken back to the Book of Judges seemingly retro-nostalgic about the sin cycle.

As you recall, each time the Israelites fell into sin, oppression was not far behind. And, the oppression was not just a nuisance. It was awful. God's people were beaten, en-slaved in most cruel ways, abused, and even killed. Families were torn apart and belongings were stolen. Young girls and their mothers were raped and brutalized. Men were often murdered. Believers were not even able to walk the streets without threat of harm. Keeping a strong faith required great courage. Deborah had this kind of strength. Many of her people did not.

Sometimes, the Israelite people just gave in to foreign beliefs in order to live somewhat peacefully, belligerently feigning disappointment in God's abandonment of them. This made it easier to disobey His commands. They tolerated, you might say. In other cases, the people of God lost their sensitivity to evil and sin due to their systematic acceptance of seemingly harmless activities rationalized as just "not that bad." To further complicate this rapid decline into paganism, the human nature of us all tends toward the grand and independent. The people began to believe that they were more than capable of designing their own values and rules. That ancient God of Adam, Abraham, Isaac, and Jacob did not serve the contemporary issues of the day. After all, it was around 1200 B.C. and the world was a happening place.

And so, oppression *happened*. Suffering abounded. Believers cried out for mercy and deliverance, and God sent relief. In the after-math of Deborah's obedience, the Israelite people enjoyed forty years of peace and, oh yes, hope. That's why we can now *re*-visit that tender outcome. But first, we must agree that oppression has, again, *happened* and that requires some framing of our situation today.

GETTING HISTORY RIGHT BEFORE WE REPEAT IT

Most serious students of history will conclude that America was discovered, founded, and colonized by Christians. I know it is considered progressive to criticize that general statement and to nit-pick around about deism, the pilgrim, minority fringe that was minimally or not religious, or to super-impose a letter written by Thomas Jefferson onto our Constitution. Notwithstanding, the historical documents, buildings, paintings, writings, journals, and original charters are gloriously drenched in references to Almighty God, the Creator, His glory, the defense of the Christian faith, and the will of the Sovereign Lord.

Those truths cannot be expunged from our nation's beginnings without gutting the combined states of the union of manuscripts, edifices, monuments, cemetery markers, churches, steeples, and works of art, archives, and authenticated historical data. The rhetoric being flung around liberal circles that America was not founded by lovers of the Christian God is very much like when one of my Kindergarten students insists that they did not steal candy from a classmate, all the while hysterically trying to wipe of the evidence from their hand and face. You see, saying something does not make it so. Evidence, proof, and the laws of logical conclusion make it so.

The phrase "separation of church and state" is not nor has it ever been in The Constitution of the United States. That concept must be spilled into the Bill of Rights by someone with a preconceived notion or a particular world view. The Ten Commandments were revered as a foundational set of human laws required to be obeyed if this new country was to be blessed by God. The behaviors required by The Commandments were first spelled out in The Holy Bible and cannot be assumed, by any serious scholar, to be part of our DNA or just something everyone knows. If you wish to quibble over whether or not America is a Christian nation founded by Christian men and women, go back to school. Say what you will about our metamorphosis since that time and I will discuss your views, but don't try your disingenuous, liberal spin on me.

Now that we are all on the same page, a calculation of the resulting outcomes from the events of the early seventeenth Century and up to the twenty-first is in order. The Mayflower Compact, The Declaration of Independence, The Articles of Confederation, and The Constitution all sought to achieve one goal; a united and strong nation where all could reach for freedom, happiness, and peace. The colonists desired to be free from the bonds of tyranny and oppression, (sound familiar?) and allowed to comport their lives, raise their families, worship their God, own their piece of the land, or direct their affairs according to the dictates of their own conscience.

Now, lest you pack a foreign concept created by the modern mindset into that last word, remember that the early settlers considered an undeniable conviction of the truth of The Bible as God's Word in order to define conscience. In other words, they desired to do what was right in God's eyes, therefore freeing their conscience to allow for their eventual success. They believed that God was on their side and endeavored to deserve His blessing.

The original Americans fought and died to achieve a small and nonintrusive government, Christian standards and education, freedom from foreign oppression and aggression, the right to life, liberty, and happiness, safety in their lands and homes, equality, fairness, justice, a firm part in the governing of the body politic, virtuous leadership, balance, privacy, personal autonomy and accountability, respect, and the intervention of blessings from God.

THAT WAS THEN. THIS IS NOW.

Here we are, just about four hundred years later, appraising the outcome, success, and current status for ourselves. Please be forewarned that I am about to infuriate *everyone*. I will try not to leave anyone out and expect to actually make myself mad, which happens all too often. At the time of this writing, we are embarking on the preparations for the 2008 Presidential elections. Indeed, by the time this book is published, the election may already be decided. I am hopeful that it will be available before many of our fellow citizens perforate random chads without conscious purpose. If not, the warnings contained herein will be crucial to America's survival anyway and are worthy of your consideration.

We are, at best, surrounded by political chaos in our land. Serious discussions revolve around opinions, experience and past performance. Hillary Clinton dug clear back into Barak Obama's Kindergarten file to disparage his suitability as a presidential candidate. (I wonder; did he color inside or outside of the lines?) The rhetoric continues with he said/she said nonsense, statements that side-step the real issues, blaming and chiding, opponent bashing, and misrepresentations of theological ideologies. There is a constant droning about reaching "across the aisles" as we watch the nation's congress define that concept as a figurative tug-of-war, each side straining to pull the opposition into the center mud puddle and getting nothing, really *nothing* done. As a result, Congress has the lowest public confidence rating in our history.

Everything, even natural disasters, is the fault of the current administration except for those things that are the fault of the current congressional majority party. Candidates are "for" something just before they are "against" it. The necessity to "look Presidential" comes up at every focus group as a big deal and darned if the contenders and their puppeteers continue to neglect the one concern paramount in the hearts and minds of the people—values, integrity, honesty, and commitment. I mean, the whole country is rolling their collective eyes so often that we are dizzy with confusion. Shake it off, people! There is a sane answer that can be demonstrated inside the voting booth by those who carry God's truth in with them, and we must be victorious before the country implodes.

Perhaps I am the only frustrated citizen out here, but I don't think so. I am a rabid consumer of anything politic, often flipping television channels for hours to get another perspective on the same story. My family considers me to be seriously flawed. So be it. Even as I mention the desire of America-loving conservatives to be apprised of the values of our elected and aspiring officials, I can hear the inane droning of the masses as they proclaim that elections are about issues, not personal values. I am stunned! Saying that we should not care about a candidate's values but only their stand on the issues is like saying it doesn't matter whether you are breathing but just that air is going in and out of your lungs. It is preposterous. As a man thinketh, so is he. Or, as it is written in the Book of Proverbs, Chapter 23, verse 7: *"For as he thinks in his heart, so is he."* Have you been quoting it without knowing from whence it came? If you hate the Bible, better stop that.

And, oh yes, a person's values are emphatically important as a determining factor that effects their future decisions. Please do not tell me what you will do about our economy. Tell me why. And, for the sake of all that is sacrosanct, stop telling me what a cad the other guy is. He or she can articulate that for themselves. Allow the liberal thinkers enough rope and there will be a hanging.

Now, remember, I am just getting warmed up here so don't get all warm and fuzzy on me if you're not mad, yet. Have you taken inventory of your personal freedoms lately or are you just so golly darn contented that our government, the justice system, our domestic agencies, and local and state officials want the best for y'all? That's the kind of lazy optimism that gets you lining up for your daily soma.

I've got a few news flashes. Your personal information is sailing in and out of unfriendly file folders along the information highway faster than light speed. Hysteria and litigation freak shows can take your freedom from you in less than an hour. Your personal property can enter the public domain at any time to make way for the better good. Free speech is defined by any tolerance censor lurking in the shadows. Your right to carry a weapon to protect yourself and your family is dwindling into a regulatory nightmare. Your children can be removed from your home by a zealot caseworker as the result of a complaint or worse, a contrived and purposeful lie. Thorough and honest investigations do not always precede incarceration. Probable cause often does not even remotely resemble probable truth. You may need to fight to fly the flag, put up a cross, pray and read your Bible, or post the Ten Commandments. The danger is real. The attack is planned, and our steadfast stand is the last hurrah.

Remember, I said that the Israelites, circa 1200 B.C. were often convinced that the mantras and hypnotic messages of their day were innocuous? I intimated that their days were filled up with compromise and rationalizations. Okay. I did not *just* suggest those circumstances since, as this writing has demonstrated, I speak my mind with un-minced words. The historical facts support the assumption that the people of God had compromised their beliefs and forgotten their promises. We are able to uncover a true picture of the chosen ones as they careened down a figurative icy slope on a rapidly accelerating sled of excuses and stubborn submissions. But, is our country and are its citizens in *that* dire of circumstances? Forgive me for what you are about to receive.

Fifty years ago, explicit underwear ads were not allowed on the television. In fact, I remember that they were not allowed under the beds of my brothers, either. Casual references to pre-marital sex, or worse, the glorification of such behavior, were considered pornography. Young unmarried women who found themselves in a "family way" were ostracized from society and became the target of gossip and furtive glances.

Boys who wore earrings or makeup had better have been in a church play. Rationalizing the need for children to have their own telephones was just crazy talk. A President of the United States who participated in tawdry and embarrassing extra-marital sexual affairs experienced a loss of respect from both parties, political and personal. The removal of sacred documents, crosses, the flag, or the words; "under God" from the fabric of our lives would have elicited gasps of horror and secretive assertions that the communists had taken over our planet.

Marriage was sacred. Childhood was sacred and protected. Religious beliefs were sacred. The unborn life was sacred. Our homes were inviolate and sacred. Inalienable rights were sacred. Good manners were expected. Fair wages and prices were considered civilized products of our society. Everyone wanted stable, whole families, predictable futures, some kind of control of the government, a say in local and community decisions, and three, square meals a day.

Don't panic! I hear you screaming epithets at the page. The 1950s *were* a time of habitual oppression of minorities, the allowance of the traumatic effects of authoritarian, and sometimes, cruel parenting, the propagation of shysters and their schemes, as well as the training ground for social and psychological concepts that would eventually lead to the celebration of an atmosphere of permissiveness that has super-charged the decline of decency as we know it.

The sick, sad world was far from perfect. But, driving down the center street of town in a '57 Chevy with the wind tossing through your hair, and the radio blasting the latest Elvis hit was sheer release. It was to experience the sublime. I will leave the pontification of the effects of those days to the scholars who pontificate such things. I merely want to point out that those days were "Leave it to Beaver" simple. And, today, we are steeping in a big pot of media filth, social dis-ease, and have compromised and rationalized ourselves into stagnant hell. On a lighter note, what a tolerant bunch we are!

HOPE SPRINGS ETERNAL

What to do? What to do? Well—this chapter is about hope. I know that, so far, it seems to elicit despair. Sorry. The first step is to recognize that we have a problem, as you know. Now that we are on the same prodigal page, consider my appeal for change.

In my first book, "Daughters of the Most High", I suggested that in order to change our lives, the first step must be to take a hard and critical look at ourselves, while asking the question: "Who am I?" or "Who are we?" Clearly, if the citizens of America are content with the direction of our nation and the society as a whole, game over. Go about your business and burn this book. You are headed that way, already.

However, I firmly believe that the signs of a reawakening are cropping up all over our country, and are spread out far enough to keep the "Firefighters for Lucifer" a few steps behind. The cries of the hopeful are gaining decibels, and just like the frantic requests of Horton who heard a Who, the invitation to increase the number of screamers is growing. How do I know? Allow me to share some news, and then make your conclusions.

I just completed facilitating some parenting trainings for a few HUD housing complexes. This is important because, first of all, they wanted the training. Folks want to do the right thing with their kids. They just don't know how. The attendees were open and willing to hear the message of personal responsibility, entertain the possibility that their values were skewed, and learn the techniques of consistency and high expectations. They see that permissiveness and tolerance have created little monsters. They want me to come back. Go figure.

Tonight my family and I will be attending the *Global* day of prayer. The events of this evening have been preceded by ten days of the fervent prayers of God's people worldwide. We are praying for peace, and wisdom, and blessing, and righteousness, and revival, and protection, and, yes, even deliverance. If you haven't participated, it's never too late to lift your voice. Please allow my parody of a cryptic sentiment from the film, "Little Big

Man": It is a good day to pray, my son. My point is that the people of God are doing their due diligence and pleading for mercy.

As a disappointed supporter of Mike Huckabee in his run for the presidency, I feel compelled to give the heads up to those who did not follow his campaign. The website and the blogs are teeming with messages of hope and out-loud commitments from solid, conservative folks across America who believe in the cause of conservatism. True, the media and the activist groups were slow to respond and not all that impressed. But, there is a housewife in the middle of America with a dishtowel draped across her breast, standing like Deborah, feet affixed, and resolved to make a difference.

There is a film-maker adorning the likes of U-tube with solid, sensible information pertaining to the attitudes and beliefs of the Huckabee fans, taking a stand. There are thousands of red-state citizens donating to the PAC established in the wake of this pivotal campaign committed to supporting the election of officials who honor the country and our founding values. Humor me and bear one more parody: We are mad *at* hell, and we're not going to take it anymore! The winds of change are blowing. What have you done for America lately?

Scores of faith-based organizations are feeding the hungry, teaching and ministering to the wounded and needy, providing housing and educational opportunities, re-inventing social systems, schools, and communities. Whatever you believe about the legacy of George W. Bush, you must acquiesce to the future impact these organizations will have.

The nation stood transfixed as we experienced collective anguish in the death of Terri Schiavo, who was allowed to starve until the burden of her life could no longer haunt us. But in its aftermath, good people have resolved to leave life and death to God, and are taking their battle to the halls of justice. In fact, the appointment of future, liberal judges to the nation's highest court will meet with un-paralleled outcry. The moral majority is poised to pounce.

Every day, random acts of kindness are happening all around us. Beneath the putrid, black smoke of frivolous lawsuits, filthy media offerings, socially repugnant behaviors in our streets, and apathetic disregard for the humane treatment of others, roils a potent brew.

A young man in Cedar City, Utah gave $109,000.00 back to the rightful owner after finding it in a bag on the college campus. A local restaurant in my town prepares a free Thanksgiving dinner for all comers every year, an act of compassion that repeats itself in every city in our country. Care workers and volunteers travel to far countries to build schools, housing, and churches. They carry with them food, water, medicines, and Bibles, often at great personal risk. Boy scouts still help old ladies across the street. I know because one helped me, recently. I am somewhat offended that he believed I was *that* old, but I thanked him, anyway.

When dogs were being abused in a recent highly-charged media event, people took the dogs in and are in the process of re-habilitation even as we speak. The same goes for the animals impacted by hurricane Katrina. Whenever loved ones go missing, complete strangers show up to search neighborhoods and surrounding areas to the exclusion of their own lives. We hear about it everyday. Believe me, all is not lost. It is just hidden from our view by evil-doers in black hats.

Until we individually accept responsibility for the terrible shape we are in, the land will grow more desolate. Deborah did not participate in some kind of internal conversation about how the commands of God were not her responsibility, or how war was a job for men only, or stay home and ease her conscience by patting herself on the back for doing her duty under a palm tree. She got up, put on the full armor of God, and rebuked a deflated Barak, putting herself in harm's way on the battlefield.

I love the story of the man visiting a third world country, washed with sadness at the scenes of starving children, filthy living conditions, and seemingly insurmountable challenges. He cries out to God: "Why, God? Why do you not send relief to these the poorest of your children?" What was the resounding answer? "I did. I sent you!"

We are the hope and it is time for another visit.

9

Political CPR

> *"The most dangerous ideas in society are not the ones being argued, but the ones that are assumed."*
>
> C. S. Lewis

As I write this particular section of the book, the 2008 primary elections for President of the United States are in full swing. The process has been discouraging, yet oddly regenerating.

It has been discouraging because the citizens of the greatest country in the world have been content to be lied to and manipulated by the media and the powerful. Several states scrambled to vie for coveted influence by holding their caucuses and primaries earlier than ever before. Members of the media spoke out brazenly in support of their favorite candidate and seemed to suffer from integrity amnesia in the reporting of balanced commentary. It was as if the whole population of our country was crippled by some kind of anxiety attack and the resultant atmosphere of fear sparked a nationwide disconnect of the collective brain trust. Here now we stand with unholy yeast coming out of our self- protecting, plugged ears.

The process has been regenerating because the very antics that have left us with a truly disturbing choice of candidates have mobilized a growing band of conservative soldiers who are ready to rumble for the sake of our godly heritage. I quote C. S. Lewis at the beginning of this chapter to remind us that the longer we keep our heads covered by poison sand, the greater the oppression that looms ahead.

The assumptive front-runners in the 2008 primary election have been touted from the airwaves, printed pages, and the misinformation highway leaving our people under-informed and cattle-prodded into line.

Conservative, value-based views have been trampled and rationalized. The Bible is about to leave the Oval office once again, beneath the arm of our forty-third President, and God's people can choose to *assume* all will be well, or they can become educated and fight back.

Deborah took on the Canaanite armies, iron chariots and all. Jael felled an evil enemy with warm milk and a tent peg. And, it is time to look to our ancestors for strength and to turn toward our God for advice. We must carefully listen to some of today's rhetoric with the understanding that figurative iron chariots can come in many models while still seeking the destruction of the people. The sounds emanating deep in the throats of the members of each political party spew out at the mere mention of the words Democrat or Republican, conservative or liberal and may require the Heimlich maneuver to clear the obstruction. No mention is made of what is good, what is right, what is moral, or what is sane. Who to hate is much more au currant than what to do.

We did have one candidate who blew in from Arkansas like a spring breeze, but believers were intimidated by pillars of flesh and have forgotten pillars of fire. Because I am ever the optimist, I will give this message another try complete with an attached disclaimer. The 2008 election is not *the* problem. It is only an illustration of the decline of our hope in Christ. *The* problem has to do with our fear, apathy, and disobedience. If you feel uncomfortable, just re-adjust that yoke atop your shoulders and read on.

RIGHTING WHAT'S WRONG

I am, most likely, now going to disparage a few sacred cows. I assure you that I mean no disrespect to the bovine of the species, but seek to expose that ignoble crowd among us, cowering behind the curtain and telling us that the very act of paying attention indicates radical intolerance. You are getting very sleepy … very sleepy … very sleepy.

On the topics of the day, Hillary Rodham Clinton has spoken and voted thus:

In October of 2000: "We must safeguard constitutional rights, including choice." In January of 2000: "Remain vigilant on a woman's right to choose." In November of 2006: "Respect Roe v. Wade, but make adoptions easier too." In June of 2007: "Lift ban on stem cell research to cure devastating diseases."

In October of 2005, Hillary voted with the liberal line on partial birth abortion and harm to the fetus. In July of 2006, she voted NO on notifying parents of minors who get out-of-state abortions. In March of 2005, she voted to approve spending one hundred million to reduce teen pregnancy through education and contraception. In March of 2004, Hillary voted NO on criminal penalty for harming unborn fetuses during other crime. She is positive about civil unions and would extend full equality of benefits. She marched in the gay pride parade in 2000. In August of 2007, she was heard to say; "If you want a winner to take on the right wing, I'm your girl." which was the follow-up pronouncement to her December 1999 warning of a ". . . vast right wing conspiracy." In July of 2007, she spoke this gem: "I consider myself a modern American progressive."[1]

Translation? Hillary is pro-murder when it comes to the unborn, pro-government when it comes to parental stewardship, pro-premarital sex and contraception, pro-gay unions, a willing harvester of unborn baby stem cells, anti-conservative and red state values, and a self-proclaimed believer in *evolving* political opinion in order to appeal to the un-educated and non-discerning voter. A "modern American progressive" believes in doing what seems right in his or her own eyes. By now, we know the danger in that doctrine and, hopefully, understand how very distant it is from the ethical standards set by our founding documents or our Sovereign founding Father.

As an equal opportunity critic, I present some of the career highlights of the new kid on the block, Barak Hussein Obama. Mr. Obama has lots of faith in the decisions made by women, gays, scientists, and the ACLU. I come to these conclusions by way of the laws of logic. Now, he is new, and therefore has been afforded lots less time to esteem himself. Still, the sultan of rhetoric has spoken and voted thus:

In August of 2007, Obama posited that stem cell research held promise to cure seventy major diseases, and that on the heels of his vote in April to expand research on more stem cell lines. April was a good month for freedom for women choosing the barbaric procedure of partial-birth abortion to solve their irresponsibility problem. It was the month of Obama's supportive assertion that women should be trusted to make the right decision when collapsing the skull of their baby to allow an easier and cleaner death. However, once your child has survived the vulnerability

1. http://ontheissues.org, last visited 10/14/07.

of the womb and delivery room, Barak Obama believes that her parents are obsolete and non sequitur. That means that your baby girl should be able to use contraception and have an out-of-state abortion without the consent of the same mother he trusted to kill her early on. At least, that was his stance in July of 2006. He does change his mind, sometimes, but mostly only when a spiritual leader begins to harm his political career and not in the case of his pro-choice, anti-family opinions.

In the month of August of 2007, he also expressed his belief that the gay rights movement is rather like the civil rights movement and that states need to strengthen civil unions. One cannot fault his consistency, however, because in June of 2006, Mr. Obama voted NO on a constitutional ban of same-sex marriage.

And then, there is this gem. Mr. Barak Hussein Obama voted NO on a Constitutional ban on the desecration of our flag while voting against Justice John Roberts and Justice Samuel Alito who both would vomit at the thought. In all fairness, Mr. Obama believes that our Constitution is a *living* document intended to be conformed to the popular beliefs of the day and would therefore support the doing of what seems right in our own eyes. I pray for an America that takes a stand in the voting booths in support of what is right in God's eyes.[2]

Now then, I could go on and on about the voting records and beliefs of every politician in Washington but that requires more self-control and intestinal fortitude than I have to spare. Suffice to say that Washington has become a den of vacillating, ear-marking, mud-slinging, finger-pointing, rationalizing demagogues who are deaf and dumb to the screams of average Americans. Peruse the internet or the library and you will see the more than disturbing trend of our elected officials to embrace the doctrines of tolerance and progressive thinking.

Why is this important? Reason would inform us that these officials have great power to affect our country and our lives. Hey, I read Ayn Rand and I must confess that the philosophy of laissez faire is compelling. Perhaps if our government would just "leave us alone," we could re-calibrate its course. In a perfect world, it might just work.

Unfortunately, the experiences of the past would indicate that when left alone, we really screw up. Remember the Israelites and the golden calf, or King Saul stepping out in the flesh without the will of God to guide, or

---

2. Ibid.

King David as he attempted to cover his sin, or Adam and Eve resolutely munching the forbidden fruit? We do not do well on our own.

Sadly, our elected officials are just a symptom of a deeper infection. Turn on the television if you are still not shaking with anxiety. Ever heard of Al Franken, or Rosie O'Donnell, or Susan Sarandon, or Jeanine Garafolo, or Michael Moore? I know you have. The hatred for our President, our country, our values, our Christian heritage, our beliefs, and our successes is palpable. Conspiracy theories are the séances of our day. Good, old-fashioned, civil disobedience has been booted out of the town square by venomous rhetoric intended to vilify and incinerate the moral majority. I invite you to consider the following examples and still remain calm.

> *"The family unit—spawning ground of lies, betrayals, mediocrity, hypocrisy, and violence—will be abolished. The family unit, which only dampens imagination and curbs free will, must be eliminated."*
>
> MICHAEL SWIFT, FEBRUARY 15, 1987

(By Swift's report, this was satire, a purging of his "inner anger" and intended for his homosexual audience.) Okay.

> *"A check will substitute for a parent's love and guidance."*
>
> BILL CLINTON,
> JANUARY 23, 1996 (PAST PRESIDENT OF US)

> *"The complete destruction of traditional marriage and the nuclear family is the 'revolutionary or utopian' goal of feminism."*
>
> KATE MILLET
> (FEMINIST WRITER AND ACTIVIST)

> *"Every child who believes in God is mentally ill."*
>
> PAUL BRANDWEIN,
> 1970 (CONSERVATIONIST)

"The life of an ant and the life of my child deserve equal consideration."

Michael W. Fox
(Senior scholar of the Humane Society)

"We have to abolish and reform the institution of marriage—By the year 2000 we will, I hope, raise our children to believe in human potential, not God—We must understand what we are attempting is a revolution, not a public relations movement."

Gloria Steinem,
March 1973 (Feminist icon)

"My books are about killing God."

Philip Pullman
(Children's Author)

"Religion is extremist. It is extreme to believe in things that your rational mind knows are not true."

Bill Maher
(Satirist and political activist)

"I don't want to be identified as someone who, at any given moment of their life, gets down to his knees and seeks whatever."

Peter Jennings
(Journalist and News Reporter)

"Fundamental, Bible-believing people do not have the right to indoctrinate their children in their religious beliefs because we are, the state, preparing them for the year 2000, when America will be part of a one-world global society and their children will not fit in."

Peter Hoagland
1983 (Democratic Congressman from Nebraska)

Political CPR

"I am convinced that the battle for humankind's future must be waged and won in the public school classroom by teachers that correctly perceive their role as proselytizers of a new faith which will replace the rotting corpse of Christianity."

JOHN J. DUNPHY
1983 (AUTHOR AND POET)

"I'm sick of talking about values, sick of pretending I have them or care more about them than I really do. Sick of bending and twisting the political causes I do care about to make them qualify as 'values'."

MICHAEL KINSLEY
(POLITICAL JOURNALIST)

"We do not need any preaching about right and wrong. The old 'thou shalts' simply are not relevant."

"Values clarification is a method for teachers to change the values of children without getting caught."

SIDNEY SIMON
(UNIVERSITY OF MASSACHUSETTS PROFESSOR AND WRITER)

"The world needs to be liberated from American values and culture, spreading across the planet as if by divine providence."

KALLE LASN
1999 (WRITER, PRODUCER, ACTIVIST)

"The truth, Dennis? Don't you know the truth is relative? Your testimony was your version of the truth. Truth is whatever you want it to be."

CRAIG LIVINGSTONE
1995 (DIRECTOR OF PERSONNEL SECURITY, CLINTON WHITE HOUSE)

> "I think I can be an honest person
> and lie about any number of things."
>
> DAN RATHER
> MAY 15, 2001 (NEWSMAN)

> "Our problem today is too little government."
>
> BARNEY FRANK
> (DEMOCRATIC POLITICIAN,
> MASSACHUSETTS HOUSE OF REPRESENTATIVES)

> "We no longer see the teaching of facts and information as
> the primary function of education."
>
> SHIRLEY MCCUNE
> 1989 (EDUCATOR, EDUCATIONAL REFORMER)

> "Children who know how to think for themselves spoil the
> harmony of the collective society which is coming, where
> everyone is interdependent."
>
> JOHN DEWEY
> (PHILOSOPHER, PSYCHOLOGIST, EDUCATIONAL REFORMER)

> "The idea that parents know what is best for their children
> is a flawed concept at best."
>
> ROBERT B. CORMANDY
> NOVEMBER 3, 1997 & DECEMBER 4, 1997
> (DIRECTOR OF PENNSYLVANIA SCHOOL COUNSELORS ASSOCIATION)

And, in the genre of humorous commentary, resides this food for thought:

> "I'm trying to organize support for a constitutional amendment to deny voting rights to born-again Christians. I feel if your citizenship is in Heaven—like a born-again Christian's is—you should give up your citizenship. Sorry but this is my new Cause. If born-again Christians are allowed to vote in this Country, then why not Canadians?"
>
> GARRISON KEILLOR
> (AUTHOR, HUMORIST, SATIRIST, RADIO PERSONALITY)

Then finally, this observation that is not at all amusing:

> *"The evaporation of four million [Christians] who believe in this crap [The Second Coming of Christ] would leave the world an instantly better place."*
>
> Andrei Codrescu
December 19, 1995
(Poet, novelist, commentator for National Public Radio)[3]

If you hate me because I believe that abortion is murder, that homosexuality is a sin, that the war in Iraq has kept America safe from further terrorist attack and championed the cause of freedom in the Middle East, that Darwinism is a futile, albeit cleverly crafted pile of garbage, that parental rights are sacrosanct, that human beings are created in God's image and therefore due more consideration that the snail darter, that global warming as a holocaust-producing event is just ridiculous and riddled with empirical folly, that we have given our liberal government way too much power, that we should drill the crap out of Anwar, that children should be disciplined to the full extent of God's recommendations, that marriage between a man and a woman is sacred, that filth and violence, pornography and addiction should be eliminated from our lives, and that I would defend to my final breath your right to disagree, then let's do coffee and *talk*.

I can show you the way to truth and peace and hope. I will listen to you, respect your thoughts, and rebuke your epithets against what is right in the eyes of God. Bring your Bible. I will be using it extensively. Don't have one? I rest my case.

The other more popular choice of your people is to burden the air ways with cursing, screaming, lying, and angry rhetoric. The apologetic of choice is to simply express a personal distaste for my opinions, and summon the worn doctrine that "everyone with any sense knows that I am a hate monger in pursuit of judgmental retribution." As a one-time friend of mine once put it; "Your Bible is not big enough for the whole world!" I submit then that my God is, and He will be making that clear shortly.

In the case that you are not numbed by this kind of philosophical shock and awe, consider some of the consequential outcroppings of progressive thought. There are more than 126,000 abortions worldwide every

---

3. http://www.aim.org/wls, last visited 10/14/07.

day. The hope of America's future was murdered at Columbine, Virginia Tech, Cleveland Elementary School, an Amish School in Pennsylvania, Hubbard Elementary School, the World Trade Center, and a meadow just outside of Shanksville, Pennsylvania.

Don't forget the court in the state of Maine that voted 7-2 in favor of giving birth control to middle school girls as young as eleven without parental notification or the college in Florida handing out condoms to the new students on campus begging the question; "What should the well-dressed student be wearing this year?"

Remember that the traditional moment of silence in the schools in Illinois at the beginning of the day has prompted a lawsuit brought by an atheist who considers this to be state-sponsored prayer, or that a law was introduced to disallow the mention of God by veterans during the flag-folding ceremony at funerals for fallen soldier, or that a mother (?) in the act of shoplifting left her baby behind in the store in order to flee the security police. And, just in case you missed it, a group of high school students in Gloucester, Massachusetts have confounded the program professionals and the local officials, en masse, after making a pact to get pregnant so they will be able to raise their terribly unfortunate babies together. P.S. The school touts a childcare center to support these very young girls for whom procreation is a "neat social game." I have to stop before I cannot.

Please hear me now. Without God, we are standing on a dual foundation; the ever-shifting sand of public policy and opinion, and our false confidence in power-hungry tyrants. This land is in the throes of a disobedient and sinful tantrum. And, truly, when Dad gets home, it will not be pretty.

10

Never Again, and This Time I Mean It!

> *"In my distress, I cried to the Lord,*
> *And, He heard me.*
> *Deliver my soul, O Lord, from lying lips*
> *And from a deceitful tongue."*
>
> PSALM 120:1–2

I WONDER IF YOU are thinking what I often do after a major upheaval in my life. I usually think about how truly stupid I must have been to have fallen for the same old lie. And, I generally follow that internal scoffing with a familiar one-two punch and renew my resolve. This kind of soul searching experience always reminds me of a volunteer position I held for about six years in our city.

In my capacity as the Chairperson for a five-county, inter-agency coordinating council, I had the occasion to spearhead, coordinate, and supervise a teen holding tank in our southern Utah city. In its heyday, St. George was the tamer but equally licentious epicenter of Spring Break debauchery in Utah. Every year, our city streets, motels, restaurants, and jail would fill up with thousands of raucous teens who had made the pilgrimage to worship the sun, the fun, and the freedom. For four, sin-packed days, the children of the damned would frolic, flirt, drink, drug, and unravel.

My part of the celebration was to oversee their stay in our makeshift retention center after their arrest and prior to their release to often furious and embarrassed parents. I would make them as comfortable as possible, give them juice, coffee, food, and lots of counsel. For some, it was a yearly habit to end up in my care. For others, the experience was a true nightmare brought on by drinking more alcohol than their weight, culminating with projectile vomiting into one of our festive, janitorial buckets. Anyway, if only I had a dollar for every time I heard this heartfelt pronouncement: "I will never do this again as long as I live. And, this time I mean it!" It is such sweet irony.

You see, the events that unfolded during the reign of Deborah, judge of Israel, did not take place inside a vacuum, devoid of rational cause or substantive history. The account of the Israelites as reported in the Book of Judges is dated around 1100–1200 B.C. Since we understand the created world to be 6–10,000 years old, (Tell it to the judge, Mr. Wizard!) the experiences of Barak, Jael, Sisera, and Deborah were occurring against the backdrop of a long line of sin-and-sin-again history. Remember that the sin cycle always ends with, "... and God was merciful and sent to his people a deliverer." It is safe to assume that the children of God have been messing up since the beginning. Perhaps, Genesis 1:26 *could* read: "And, God said, 'Let us make man in Our own image... *and it all went downhill from there!*'"

LEARNING FROM THE PAST

It is not my intention to further depress and discourage. Rather, the focus of these historical examples is for the purpose of creating our strategy. As it pertains to my premise, the mistakes of the past do, indeed, frame the decisions of the future. Though not an exhaustive study, here presented is an illustrative laundry list of Biblical accounts that support the thesis.

After the demise of the oldest guys ever, the prophet Noah arrived on the scene. And then, one of the oddest concepts written of in the Bible occurs. We learn of a "super race" of supposed heroes called the Nephilim. The text indicates that these "sons of God" pro-created with the daughters of men and produced offspring. If that is not an example of the unequal yoke, I stand down.

Anyway, it is no surprise that the next part of the text explains that men became so wicked that "... *every* inclination of the thoughts of his heart was *only* evil *all* the time." (Genesis 6:5)

Dear Lord, I pray we are not there, yet! End of scene: total annihilation. Cut to next scene.

Noah's boys and all of their progeny take the opportunity to spread across the globe, not-withstanding a little confusion created at their "heavenly tower." Tribes and civilizations are formed. The earth begins its renewal. We should not be amazed that philosophies, and religions, and myths, and tyrants who followed other gods began to swirl about the earth. The God who was the architect of the great flood was not so much fun. They needed variety. They needed freedom. They needed self-expression. By the way, it's just funny to note that they did not champion tolerance. In fact, the tribes hated each other and many of their descendants do to this day. I think they were a little more honest in their wickedness than we are.

Here I find sweet irony (just because of the name) in the account of a feller named Nimrod, a descendant of Ham, and his animation of the great Babylonian empire along with his founding of another well-known city, Ninevah. Both cities would later become the recipients of a violent end. But, not only did Ham begat the line of Nimrod, he fathered the nations of Canaan and all the other "—ites." And, guess who was calling the nasty shots in the time of our heroine, Deborah? And, that knowledge affords us a little flash forward to an example of resultant consequences. 'Nuf said.

Forgive my digression. After the cleansing of the planet by an angry God, the survivors of the flood inter-married (often as captives), set up their own priests, created designer gods, and proceeded to oppress and be oppressed. This is sounding familiar.

Along comes Abram, from the line of Shem, another of Noah's baby boys. He sets out, in obedience to God, with his drop-dead gorgeous wife, Sarai and nephew, Lot for the land of Canaan. Famine forces a change of course. They end up in Egypt where Abram's godly resolve *dis*solves and he places the lovely Sarai into jeopardy to save his own neck.

Back they go to Bethel where family bickering and fighting and regional battles rage. Abram and Lot head north and, lo and behold, the sister cities of Sodom and Gomorrah begin to unravel. That account is world renowned in its revelation of sinful living.

God reveals future blessings to Abram, promising a son from his loins. Wouldn't it be lovely if that promise had insulated him from all ill? It was not to be. Unable to wait on the Lord, Abram slid into a convenient yoke with the family maid, all of which set into motion the obliteration of an entire race. I'm sure that won't happen to us.

Abram, of course, goes on to do great things in honor and obedience to the Lord after being promised to be the blessed father of many nations. Name change and that's a wrap, right? Not exactly. The Lord formulates a kind of pre-test to assure that all of the nonsense is behind them. Mercifully, God refines Abraham's obedience by way of a gotcha technique that could have cost him a son.

Nevertheless, the whole Jacob and Easu drama dangerously rocks the boat and the unfairness of it all still causes umbrage in Bible studies, today. The sons of Jacob filled with jealousies and evil by-pass the whole brotherly love thing and send Joseph up the river. He eventually saves their sorry skins, along with the whole starving lot. And, it is beginning to look like a carnival merry-go-round that I want to get off of. That is just in the first book of the Bible.

To spare the pain of continuing, let's just agree that the history of the world along with its subsequent civilizations is fraught with the repetitive failures of God's people to obey His commands given to them since the beginning of Creation. The results have been a consistent and historically documented pattern of the people doing what is right in their own eyes, falling into the evil behaviors hated by God, suffering with oppression and darkness, and feebly crying out for deliverance. Good grief! Will we ever learn?

CAN I GET A WITNESS?

Just for fun (?), we should try to connect the dots. We live in a blessed land wherein opportunities abound and national strength is renowned, worldwide. The empire is alive and well. We are different from the pre-flood miscreants. We are not Babylon, or Rome, or Sodom and Gomorrah, or Ninevah, or Pompeii, or Nazi Germany. WE are America, the land of the free and the home of the brave. And, anyway the peoples of the earth have developed into an ominous force. The proposal that all will be brought down is just an outrage, perhaps just the ramblings of another apocalyptic psychopath. I thank you very much.

But, are we really just puking into the retention center bucket, reciting a tired resolve, and chomping at the bit to get back out and do it all over again? Humor me for a moment and entertain this little "what if."

Say that the United States of America has reached critical mass in the area of dwindling values, forced compromises, the marketing of graphic and boundary-less filth, the murder of the weak and vulnerable, clandestine plots to oppress, kill, and destroy, government graft, police misconduct, court system takeovers, constant persecution of Christians and Christianity, compounding addictions, the sacrifice of our children to a supposed idyllic lifestyle, educational brainwashing, the deification of anything other than God, and a general, national belief that all is well as long as we all get along, tolerating the whole lot, free of judgmental criteria. I suppose it could be said that we could be unstoppable just as soon as doing what seems right in our individual worldview becomes the mandate. Scared yet?

Maybe you are still all flowered-up and hoping the sky is *not* falling. I will never cease praying for you, as long as this new world is a distant threat and not pummeling my front door with a battering ram.

If you are steamed, or concerned, or frightened, or just resolved, make a plan. "What if" it could happen again? "What if" we really are in trouble? "What if" the United States of America is teetering on the brink of disaster? "What if" that puny, old Bible *is* big enough for the whole world? I beg you to take this warning to heart. It was originally intended for the Israelites, announcing the coming judgment and their resultant exile. It is as salient today as an over-lay for comparison. Take heed.

> *"To whom shall I speak and give warning that they may hear? Indeed their ear is uncircumcised, and they cannot give heed. Behold the word of the Lord is a reproach to them; they have no delight in it. Therefore I am full of the fury of the Lord. I am weary of holding it in. I will pour it out on the children outside, and on the assembly of young men together; for even the husband shall be taken with the wife the aged of him who is full of days. And their houses shall be turned over to others, fields and wives together; for I will stretch out My hand against the inhabitants of the land" says the Lord. "Because from the least of them even to the greatest of them, everyone is given to covetousness. And from the prophet even to the priest, everyone deals falsely. They have also healed the hurt of My people slightly, saying, 'Peace, peace!' when* **there** *is no peace. Were they ashamed when they had committed abomination? No! They were not at all ashamed; nor did they know how to blush. Therefore they shall fall among those who fall; at the time I punish them, they shall be cast down, says the Lord."*
>
> JEREMIAH 6:10–13

If those words do not give you pause, try these:

> *"Son of man, when a land sins against Me by persistent unfaithfulness, I will stretch out my hand against it; I will cut off its supply of bread, send famine on it, and cut off man and beast from it . . . as I live, says the Lord God, they would deliver neither sons nor daughters, only they (Noah, Daniel, and Job) would be delivered, and the land would be desolate."*
>
> Ezekiel 14:13, 16b

If you are reading this book as a saved child of God, the calling is sure. It is time for action. It is time to approach the judge at the gate. It is time to stand in the gap. It is time to call the faint hearted to action. And, this time, I mean it!

11

That the Nation May Endure

*"It is when a people forget God
hat tyrants forge their chains."*

PATRICK HENRY

*"Men must be governed by God
or else they will be ruled by tyrants."*

WILLIAM PENN

I RECOGNIZE HOW UNPOPULAR the subject of this book may be in today's sophisticated world. We are a nation of affluence, and regardless of the price of gasoline, a nation of excess.

As I have already shared with you, the students at our school and childcare often arrive at the beginning of their day with soda pop, candy, donuts, toaster pastries, etc. What I have not shared with you is the concern I feel for the health and safety of each of the children. Every day we prepare breakfast, snacks, and lunch for the whole lot, and every day I carry ponderously heavy trash bags filled to the bursting with rejected food out to the bin. I will often take a mental flight of fancy and imagine bringing those wasted items to starving children in far-away countries just to see their expression of gratitude.

Oh sure, there has always been an attitude of ingratitude among children, though I have heard stories about those who grew up in agrarian America who ate what they were given and expressed thanks. And, I have heard stories of children in the early days of our country who received whittled toys and stuffed sock dolls for gifts and responded with screams of joy, cherishing those items always.

The unpopular point that I am attempting to make is that somehow we believe that our lives are holistically better because we have *more*. Yes, I am grateful for medicines, and sanitation techniques, and swifter exchanges of information, and technological breakthroughs. I do not wish to banish all signs of modern convenience and live a life of poverty and forced self-reliance. Our choice is not between two excessive ends of the scale. It is always humorous to me that an argument between a conservative and a liberal often teeters between the ridiculous far right and the ludicrous far left.

Anyway, the suggestion that early America had something to covet may conjure up visions of bat wings, eye of newt, and puritanical undergarments. That is not what I am suggesting. I am, in fact, drawing a direct allusion to the things we have left behind, like respect for our elders, or gratitude for our bounty, or appreciation of our freedoms, or an obedient fear of our Creator. We got a taste of it after the events of 9-11. Flags hung from every possible appendage and pole. Neighbors reached out to each other in a show of solidarity. Churches experienced an influx of errant members. And, our President made a firm resolve that those dead shall not have died in vain, amidst the roar of a cheering crowd.

BRAINSTORMING A CHANGE THAT LASTS

Exit the threat. Enter the apathy and, in the end, outrage. The only problem is that the outrage is no longer leveled against the terrorists or the self-proclaimed haters of Americans. No-o-o, now the frantic voices cry "foul!" George W. Bush is a daily target of attack by those who would have us forget the laws of a logical argument. One of the latest hysterical positions taken is that we should exert force against Iran and North Korea. And, out of the other side of their mouths, comes the message that exerting force in Iraq was wrong, wrong, wrong. Sorry, Mr. President. Damned if you do. Damned if you don't.

In order to right all of our nation's wrongs, Nancy Pelosi traveled to the Middle East to extend a little smile and a word of encouragement to our enemies. Barak Obama wants to rush over there and just speak peace and love into their lives. Liberal Hollywood wants us to stay home, turn out the lights, and leave the neighbors alone. They are longing for the Bible to leave the White House so the nation can get back to doing what seems right in its own eyes, right *in* the Oval Office.

The left-leaners want us to step aside and let the United Nations do its best. By the way, that is the same United Nations that poured Oil for Food money down several foreign rat holes. The United Nations doesn't like the U.S. They heartily disagree with our "imperialist aggressor" mentality. They meet in cities across the world to form little resistance groups with the intent of blocking our goals while keeping the phone lines open in order to request our help, financial assistance, and military acumen. I don't want to be the Chicken Little here, but the sky is falling and we are un-equally yoked!

And, just in case the yoke you bear is not uncomfortable enough, be aware that here at home, liberal judges and militant legal and public agencies, including our police force, have a disdain for disagreement of any kind. While I do not support the beliefs of polygamist factions, children were unlawfully and undiplomatically ripped from their homes without certifiable, probable cause. We shoot first and ask questions later.

Have you ever tried to exert a logical request on a government agency? I was astounded to receive this curt answer: "We do not have to be logical. We just follow the rules." In this case, the rule was so insignificant that even one of my Kindergarten students remarked; "That's just crazy!" And, it was.

In my case, I throw bags of food away because a government agency says I must. I place children in a regulated area for play where their creativity and the joy of outside play is stifled because a government agency says I must. I am required to deify the schedule above the needs of a child, because a government agency says I must. I pay for products and equipment I will never use because, well, you know. Small business owners are un-equally yoked.

Clearly, the most transparent example of self-inflicted bondage is the same trend in our culture that was sinking Deborah's. It is now considered at the least intolerant and at its fiercest a hate crime to advise your children to marry within his or her religion. It was a command given to the Israelites that, when ignored, led to idol worship, immorality, and oppression.

Today, marriage has become such a whim that young couples are convinced that what used to be a sacred, lifetime commitment can be exchanged like a bad Christmas present. If one makes a mistake, it can always be righted in divorce court, often without any contest, and sometimes via the internet!

God is the same yesterday, today, and always. His Word is perfect. Marriages end because today's couples enter lightly and without expectations. 'Til death us do part has been neologized to mean 'til I disagree with you, or 'til you bug me, or 'til I'm tired of you. Getting the right color of flowers for the wedding has become much more important than choosing the right mate. Oppression comes in all the latest colors. Praying together and staying together only comes in true blue. (Little joke.)

By the way, do we really think that a failed marriage only hurts two people? Get an abacus. Your counting skills are way off.

And, while we are on the subject of families, what shall we do with shattered ones? Dads are bailing on their responsibilities, moms are leaving home at a startling rate, children are entering and leaving juvenile and foster systems through whirling turnstiles, irresponsible and illogical state employees are hijacking kids while the church shrugs off the burden, parents are impotent to keep their little ones under control in public places, weary grandparents are pulling bunk beds into their guest rooms for returning grand-children bludgeoned by drug-addicted, alcoholic, irresponsible, or lazy parents, and our best answer is to bring in the secular authorities. Is this what is right in our own eyes?

Not enough for you? Let's take on a huge sacred cow, shall we? What has the government done for you, lately? As I write this, our United States Congress is at its all-time lowest approval rating *ever*! These are *our* representatives, get it? Do they represent you, or do they represent special interests, pet projects, personal investments, and liberal hype? Yes. I *am* referring to environmentalists and their like. *This* is my Father's world. It is not the property of the Kennedy compound.

In Deborah's day, the prevailing power was in the hands of violent factions who hated God's people. The Israelites were unsafe in the public square or traveling the roads. They were a constant source of worry for the local thugs in power because they just kept having babies and growing in numbers, so they were the object of genocide whenever possible.

Listen to me. People are more important than animals. Peter Singer would not agree, nor would Robert Kennedy, nor would the Earth Liberation Front, nor would your not-so-friendly neighborhood atheists. God gave man the assignment to be a steward of the earth. We must protect it, sure, and make good decisions with integrity. No matter what William Shatner (whose work I love) says, over-population is *not* our problem. Surely, we are not about to repeat the folly of ancient Israel?

I could go on all day about big government and liberal death squads, but I can't take it all in without sensing impending brain hemorrhage. We the people are systematically losing our representation, our freedoms, our control, our voice, and our sanctity. I am reminded of a political cartoon, circa late 1600s of a huge King George, reveling in the bounty provided by the suffering pilgrims. Revolution, anyone? No? Well then, how about we just agree that oppression is happening?

Forget foreign governments and terrorists that want to kill us. We are just as terrorized by the FDA, the CPS, Homeland Security, a vile and cancerous judicial system, broken borders, explosive crime rates, and the list is endless. I, for one, long for pure reconciliation, the likes of which was once located between two palms. Oh, I hope a Ten Commandments memorial was not positioned in *that* place! Never mind. That was probably okay. Tsk, tsk, says enlightened America. And so, we worship at the altar of government, regulation, tolerance, environmentalism, science, secular progressivism, and liberal thought. We embrace disease models to explain away sin, soil our minds and those of our children with filth from media and entertainment, sell our souls for a coveted idol, turn away from morality and goodness, rationalize our life's choices, and murder infants and otherwise vulnerable citizens.

Disease and disaster is rampant across the planet, persecutions and ethnic cleansings are commonplace, and economic disaster is poised to descend.

Add to all of this merriment, shysters preaching an abridged gospel, naming it and claiming it, reciting formulated chants and prayers, and victimizing the weaker brethren. Or, for a real treat, round up the gang and toddle off to the local seeker friendly church where the Word of God is considered divisive and intolerant and just not as much fun as a puppet show. Still think we are doing great? I beg you to consider the following.

> *"These six things the Lord hates,*
> *Yes, seven are an abomination to Him:*
> *A proud look,*
> *A lying tongue,*
> *Hands that shed innocent blood,*
> *A heart that devises wicked plans,*
> *Feet that are swift in running to evil,*
> *A false witness who speaks lies,*
> *And one who sows discord among brethren."*
>
> PROVERBS 6:16–19

> "The fear of the Lord is to hate evil;
> Pride and arrogance and the evil way
> And the perverse mouth I hate.
> Counsel is mine, and sound wisdom;
> I am understanding, I have strength."
>
> PROVERBS 8:13–14

> "The fear of the Lord is the beginning of wisdom,
> And the knowledge of the Holy One is understanding."
>
> PROVERBS 9:10

> "Let us hear the conclusion of the whole matter:
> Fear God and keep His commandments,
> For this is man's all.
> For God will bring every work into judgment,
> Including every secret thing,
> Whether good or evil."
>
> ECCLESIASTES 12:13–14

> "If you are willing and obedient,
> You shall eat the good of the land;
> But, if you refuse and rebel,
> You shall be devoured by the sword"; . . .
>
> ISAIAH 1:19–20A

> "Woe to those who call evil good, and good evil,
> Who put darkness for light, and light for darkness;
> Who put bitter for sweet, and sweet for bitter!
> Woe to those who are wise in their own eyes,
> And prudent in their own sight!
> Woe to men mighty at drinking wine,
> Woe to men valiant for mixing intoxicating drink,
> Who justify the wicked for a bribe,
> And take away justice from the righteous man!"
>
> ISAIAH 5:20–23

> "But it shall come to pass, if you do not obey the voice of the Lord your God, to observe carefully all His commandments and His statues which I command you today, that all these curses will come upon you and overtake you: Cursed shall you be in the city, and cursed shall you be in the country. Cursed shall be your basket and your kneading bowl. Cursed shall be the fruit of your body and the produce of your land, the increase of your cattle and the offspring of your flocks. Cursed shall you be when you come in, and cursed shall you be when you go out. The Lord will send you cursing, confusion, and rebuke in all that you set your hand to do, until you are destroyed and until you perish quickly, because of the wickedness of your doings in which you have forsaken Me."
>
> DEUTERONOMY 28:13–20

Finally, with trembling hand I share this imposing warning.

> "To whom shall I speak and give warning,
> That they may hear?
> Indeed their ear is uncircumcised,
> And they cannot give heed.
> Behold the word of the Lord is reproach to them;
> They have no delight in it.
> Therefore I am full of the fury of the Lord.
> I am weary of holding it in.
> I will pour it out on the children outside,
> And on the assembly of young men together;
> For even the husband shall be taken with the wife,
> The aged of him who is full of days."—
> 'Thus says the Lord: Stand in the ways and see
> And ask for the old paths, where the good way is.
> And walk in it.
> Then you will find rest for your souls.
> But they said, "We will not walk in it."
> Also I set watchmen over you, saying,
> 'Listen to the sound of the trumpet!'
> But they said, "We will not listen.'
> Therefore hear, you nations,
> And know, O congregation, what is among them,
> Hear, O earth!
> Behold, I will certainly bring calamity on this people—"
>
> JEREMIAH 6:10–11, 16–19A

12

The Sum of the Parts

"Sum: the aggregate of two or more numbers, magnitudes, quantities, or particulars, as determined by the mathematical process of addition; total."

THE RANDOM HOUSE COLLEGE DICTIONARY,
1973 EDITION

As my husband often wails at me; "What's the point?" Now, even though that may seem rude, it is an appropriate question. If I left you with no denouement, so to speak, the whole exercise may be a waste of time, and I am not in the business of squandering my already limited hours on earth. To that end, I offer the following suggestions:

Seek the truth. In that statement reside just three, little words. Regrettably, in the hearts and minds of Americans, four other words cower in silence: What *is* the truth? We have been too long a willing audience of the screamers and schemers. The hypnotic opinions of the earth dwellers bombard us from the cradle to the grave.

In our public agencies, the truth has been replaced by the sanctity of the system. Government social workers follow the agency profile and levy according to the charts. Teachers dare not violate the approved core curriculum. Local officials refer to "the plan" even in cases of ridiculous, out-dated regulations. Have you tried to refute an incorrect ordinance, lately? Oil your rifle. The tanks are coming through the living room.

Our foundation has crumbled, and we sit idly by letting the last vestiges of our freedom get tied up in the utter travesty of our court system. The only answer really is to seek the truth. But, in order to perform this seemingly insurmountable task, we have got to slap our own faces and wake up. An exchange of ideas is only as effective as the depth of the pool.

If you do not study, read, listen, question, and research a thing, it will overtake you with its agenda.

A FEW NON-EXAMPLES

I am, right now, conjuring memory footage of Barak Obama verbally fantasizing a new world, designed by him, produced by him, and engineered by him. As I experience his brilliant rhetoric, it is clear that Mr. Obama truly believes that if he *says* it, it is true. And, I watch in terrified awe as audiences take it in without as much as an askance glance, tears welling up and all.

Today, he postulated that the Middle East, which has been in constant turmoil since the door opened on the Ark, will be caught under his spell and all will live in peace and harmony. The Jews beg to differ, as their back porches open to a dangerous and forever stormy land. And, just as Deborah tiptoed around the countryside in ancient times to avoid falling into the hands of marauding Philistines so go the lives and times of the modern Israelis.

Ex-President Jimmy Carter, who could never seem to accomplish anything worthy of the history books, went right over there, sat down with bonafide terrorist organization leaders, and charmed the heck out of them. That worked.

Saying it, or hoping it, or dreaming it *will not* accomplish it. Do we understand, I mean *truly* understand the conflict? The Middle East is not solely a twenty-first century drama. Have you studied the ancient world, read the Word of God as history, or sought wisdom and information from those who have labored or lived there? You stand naked and vulnerable awaiting marching orders, without strategy and knowledge. Fox News, CNN, radio gurus, political pundits, and dishonorable men will herd you into the stiles and thump your head with a mechanical rod. At least, there will be nothing in your head to lose.

Be aware, Deborahs of today! The basis of truth is God's infallible Word. It is pregnant with history, truth, wisdom, strategy, example, rebuke, warnings, and prophecies. It was Deborah's only reference apart from her relationship with Yahweh. You would do well to read, assimilate, follow and preach it. Tell your men friends. They may be worried about chariots of destruction, and cannot see the apocalypse for the stage show. In the sacred name of Jesus, at least tell your children. They seem to be more open to wisdom and information.

EDUCATION IS THE ANSWER

Seek truth. That's the first blade to hone. As a companion in your quest, I entreat you to *never, never cease learning*. That would seem to be part and parcel of seeking the truth, but somehow, the two concepts get stacked up over the airport with one incoming and another crash landing. It is a far too common state of human nature for us to stick to the old ways of doing things, without ever questioning our beliefs. That one exercise, alone, could change lives dramatically.

Allow me to illustrate. When I first moved to southern Utah, I noted a provocative and dangerous local attitude. Often when driving to my destination, I would be cast into a real-life video game experience. Several vehicles would turn into my path, without so much as a wave of the hand, a signal light, or even any audible warning. When I inquired of the locals about this vexing situation, I was told: "Oh, those guys. They do that same thing every day at the same time." Apparently, it was my charge to avoid the time-honored right-of-way tradition.

The town has grown significantly since those days, and to drive in that manner would certainly get one killed. So, either those guys are no longer with us, or they have learned something new. To accept a way of thinking or completing tasks simply because it is the only way you know, is suicide. The Bible tells us to; "Test all things, hold fast what is good."(1 Thessalonians 5:21) Even in the simplest of choices lies a possible poison dart. Just run you hands through my junk drawer at home if you don't believe me.

Being a lifelong learner and a seeker of truth can light the way for other seekers. "Thy Word is a lamp unto my feet, and a light unto my path."(Psalm 119:105)

DO AS I SAY AND NOT AS I DO

Live an honorable life. The scripture speaks often of honor. We are called to honor our god, our husbands, our wives and families, our neighbors, our contracts, our governments, and our commitments. Honor is a tricky little bit of business. First, it is difficult to determine, without some sort of criteria, what is worthy of this great endowment. And next, the challenge becomes determining who and what fits the criteria.

Of course, I would recommend the greatest litmus test ever written, the words of the Bible.

> *"But now the Lord says: Far be it from Me; for those who honor Me I will honor, and those who despise Me shall be lightly esteemed."*
>
> 1 SAMUEL 2:30B

> *"Pray for us; for we are confident that we have a good conscience, in all things desiring to live honorably."*
>
> HEBREWS 13:18

> *"Honor all people. Love the brotherhood. Fear God. Honor the King."*
>
> 1 PETER 2:17

> *"Be kindly affectionate to one another with brotherly love, in honor giving preference to one another."*
>
> ROMANS 12:10

> *"Therefore as we have opportunity, let us do good to all, especially those who are of the household of faith."*
>
> GALATIANS 6:10

As I often tell my students, there is very little comfort in the beauty of a thing if it cannot be trusted to remain true. In fact, more often than not, beauty and the beast can be one and the same. Don't believe me? Read "The Portrait of Dorian Gray." After which, you can sleuth out the people you know that may have a rather gnarly looking painting hidden in the closet. Or, better yet, refer to the words of Christ. *"A good tree cannot bear bad fruit, nor can a bad tree bear good fruit. Every tree that does not bear good fruit is cut down and thrown into the fire. Therefore, by their fruits you will know them."*(Matthew 7:18-20) Therefore, if a man's behavior does not produce real and honorable fruit, quickly question his integrity.

What has our government done for you, lately? Or, an even more vital question to ask yourself may be; what are the core beliefs of your candidate for political office? Are there any signs of unfinished or questionable decisions left in his wake? Who does he or she admire, hang out with, look to for inspiration, invite to the bargaining table, or sign on with in business? You must measure their choices, their voting records, some of their personal judgments, the character of their associates, and the integrity of their spouses. You must use the barometer of God's Word. I know that is very incorrect, politically. So be it.

In its final refining, honor is the ability to esteem someone or something more than oneself. I know what the therapists out there are thinking. Just hear me out. There is nothing wrong with self-sacrifice, heroism, and worship as long as the recipient is honorable in his, her, or its own right. Honor is earned and commanded. If you are a Deborah of today, you *must* know it when you see it. Study it. Live it. Expect it and fight to bring it back to our land. Moving on.

WE CANNOT DO THIS FROM THE SOFA

Work HARD and NEVER give up. This is best exemplified with a story. Jesus often used stories. He called them parables. In the book of Luke, chapter 18, we find the parable of a woman. Were she an actual person, I would find her to be worthy of having her name engraved on the plaque along with Deborah, and Ruth, and Rahab, and Jael. It is written:

> *"Then He spoke a parable to them, that men always ought to pray and not lose heart, saying: There was in a certain city a judge who did not fear God nor regard man. Now there was a widow in that city and she came to him, saying, Get justice for me from my adversary. And he would not for a while; But afterward he said within himself, Though I do not fear God nor regard man, yet because this widow troubles me I will avenge her, lest by her continual coming she weary me."*
>
> LUKE 18:1–5

How can we draw relevant direction from this carefully crafted teaching moment? Well—Those of you who have not had the pleasure of dealing with a judge who neither fears God nor cares about you are truly leading a charmed existence. Duck and bob, and *do not* get into a situation with the legal system. It is an exercise in exponential futility if you are hoping for justice. Hard work is a colossal understatement. Never giving up is tantamount to sainthood.

The law is the law is the law. Oh yes, it changes with the local authorities, legislative ineptitude, and subjective interpretation. I dare you to fight that and end up with anything resembling the truth. The dedicated woman of this parable would have been respected for her faith by the citizens of the day. The situation was not better under the tyrannical rule of Rome, the Sanhedrin, or any non-believer. Remember, the early Christians were hated and vilified. When I think of the bravado suggested, I feel weak. Still, she worked hard and did not give up. That will be your great task as our proposed estrogen army steps out to save our country.

I also cannot help remembering a dear student I have. Looking at her, you would immediately be drawn by the elfin shape of her face and large, expressive, moppet eyes. The under-lying melancholy of her story includes a diagnosis of a genetic syndrome that may very well end her life early or, at best, seriously undermine the quality of it. I know our God is good, and I trust His creation, but do not understand, in my sinful state, the reason for this sorrowful situation.

Anyway, the news is certainly not all bad. The beautiful child to whom I refer is, all at once, the most fascinating and enchanting person I know. Though she struggles with even the simplest of academic tasks, her will to accomplish them is unparalleled. I have watched in awe as she manipulates a toy with doors or switches until her goal is met, no matter how long it takes or how frustrating the completion of it may be. This is her work and she performs it with the integrity of a saint.

Work HARD and NEVER give up. Our work is most assuredly cut out for us in the land flowing with milk and honey. But, if we give up when the policies seem unchangeable, or stop trying when our message falls on deaf (and dumb) ears, we become a part of the machine. Christian women CAN be heard. I have heard you *be* heard. You must write and call your congressmen. You have to vote. You are honor-bound to model what you preach and teach to your children. And, I know you can certainly craft a way to motivate mere men. Oh boy, am I on the short list, now.

BE PROUD OF OUR COUNTRY

Remember who you are. Don't apologize. Never compromise. While I could certainly speak volumes on each of these concepts, there has been much presented already in earlier chapters. I speak of these things now just to shore up the proverbial levee.

As I watch some of the international shenanigans euphemized as diplomacy across the globe, I am convinced that America is shamed. Please note that I did not say **a**shamed. Though I think there are radical factions of the citizenry who *are* ashamed of this country, I doubt they are still reading this book. I fancy I lost them at the introduction.

So, for those of you who are still reading, perhaps hoping to be redeemed for your choice to continue, we have been *shamed* by an insidious under-current of anti-patriotism and an even more far-reaching web of propaganda. There are those inside and outside of our borders who would have us believe that America is the Great Satan. They label us aggressors. They consider us to be arrogant. They call us wasteful and inconsiderate, selfish, and hateful. Those are just a few examples. Now, when I was a child, that kind of name-calling came from the bad kids, not the nice kids. I was taught to share, be helpful, respect my elders, take responsibility, and love one another. Shame on me!

Contrasted with countries over-run with examples of genocide, ethnic cleansing, Islamic jihad, prohibition of the simplest of freedoms, bullets and rockets whizzing past the marketplaces, country-sides pockmarked by mass graves, purposeful starvation, terrorist factions leveling high-powered weaponry at each other, uranium-enriching psychopaths, and tyrannical (and certifiably crazy) despots, America is doing a marvelous job. Why are we so despised?

Well—America doesn't always do the right thing. Sorry. We screw up. Often, we do what seems right in our own eyes. And, ever since we kicked God out of the public square, we are screwing up more and more. A very good suggestion to alleviate this vile circumstance would be to *remember who we are*. I've already discussed our founding principles, documents, and fathers. Quickly, we forget and just as quickly, we forge our own chains. It used to be thus:

> *"Our Constitution was made only for a moral and religious people—so great is my veneration of the Bible that the earlier my children begin to read, the more confident will be my hope that they will prove useful citizens in their country and respectful members of society."*
>
> JOHN ADAMS

> *"Only a virtuous people are capable of freedom. As nations become corrupt and vicious, they have more need of masters."*
>
> BENJAMIN FRANKLIN

"To the kindly influence of Christianity we owe that degree of civil freedom, and political and social happiness which mankind now enjoys . . . Whenever the pillars of Christianity shall be overthrown, our present republican forms of government, and all blessings which flow from them, must fall with them."

JEDEDIAH MORSE

"We profess to be republicans, and yet we neglect the only means of establishing and perpetuating our republican forms of government, that is, the universal education of our youth in the principles of Christianity by the means of the Bible. For this Divine Book, above all others, favors that equality among mankind, that respect for just laws, and those sober and frugal virtues, which constitute the soul of republicanism."

BENJAMIN RUSH

"If we and our posterity reject religious instruction and authority, violate the rules of eternal justice, trifle with the injunctions of morality, and recklessly destroy the political constitution which holds us together, no man can tell how sudden a catastrophe may overwhelm us that shall bury all our glory in profound obscurity."

DANIEL WEBSTER

"Men, in a word, must necessarily be controlled either by a power within them or by a power without them; either by the Word of God or by the strong arm of man; either by the Bible or by the bayonet."

ROBERT WINTHROP

"Of the many influences that have shaped the United States into a distinctive nation and people, none may be said to be more fundamental and enduring than the Bible."

RONALD REAGAN

> *And, this from the First Chief Justice of the US Supreme Court that surely brings tears to the eyes of any American concerned about future appointments to that powerful body:*
>
> *"Unto Him who is the author and giver of all good, I render sincere and humble thanks for His manifold and unmerited blessings, and especially for our redemption and salvation by His beloved son. He has been pleased to bless me with excellent parents, with a virtuous wife, and with worthy children. His protection has companied me through many eventful years, faithfully employed in the service of my country; His providence has not only conducted me to this tranquil situation but also given me abundant reason to be contented and thankful. Blessed be His holy name!"*
>
> CHIEF JUSTICE JOHN JAY

That is a true picture of our county's foundation. Today, our kids are even afraid to read the Bible at recess. You *can* use the name of God, of course, as long as it is "a swear," a terminology I use with my younger students. I dare you to go and listen to the masses on the public school playgrounds and come home uplifted and hopeful.

Just to remain consistent, I would like to shine possibly a new light on the account of Deborah, in that old, dusty Bible. I am referring to Judges 4:9–21 as my proof text. Do not under any circumstance ascertain that I engage in my own, little embellishment of the true text. That may border on heresy sometimes, and I am not in that business. I'm referring to the actual account and the logical and factual outcome of the recorded events. I wonder if anyone, besides me, has noted any sub-text that supports the recommendation to remember who we are.

I have simply noted that as Barak was self-talking the command of God into a strategic fear-for-all, the backstage drama was unfolding exactly according to plan. Deborah was sizing up her information and preparing to rebuke the trembling troop leader, but also, Heber, the Kenite was making a decision to pitch his family tents in the direct, but safely distant proximity of Mt. Tabor. And, his wife, Jael, was hanging the goat milk bladder on a multi-use tent peg.

We would do well to *remember who we are* in the eyes of a loving Heavenly Father, also. Do you really believe that your excellent driving skills, or your careful nutritional choices, or a super-natural perception of dangerous situations has kept you from violent or deadly harm all these years? You've got to be kidding. Our God keeps you until the very moment he takes you. That is a sobering truth.

And, all the while you are architecturally *designing* your next clever move, God, the great architect, is *moving* your next deadly design. Stop praying for traveling mercies if you don't believe it. Or, realize that you are special in the eyes of a loving Father, and that He has called you to step out at such a time as this.

But since the Bible is not big enough for the whole world, as my angry friend once vomited, Americans may be more comfortable with this quote:

> "If God is dead, all things are permitted."
> DOSTOEVSKY'S "GRAND INQUISITOR"

You see why I say we must remember who we are? Further, we must not apologize for our beliefs, our Christian standards, or God's Word. And, any compromise of those basic principles grants permission to the enemies of God's people to polish up the iron chariots and storm our cities. Four of those figurative iron chariots, stolen from our own stock, murdered over three thousand of our friends and neighbors in September of 2001. Then, we did not stand ashamed of our land. Then, we stood united and resolved. Where have all the heroes gone? I guess they are just waiting for the arrival of the heroine(s). And, we cannot wait any longer, ladies. The barbarians are at the gate.

REMEMBER TO PAY IT FORWARD

A true heroine must *experience sacrifice and charity*, love their neighbor, and pay it forward. I do not know if the world as we know it will be here for our children's children or their children. I *do* know that all of this will end some day. In fact, if you have read the book of Revelation, the end is coming shortly. And, though the final drama is certain, portending the truly horrific, there is no reason to hold back on the great commission. By the very nature of understanding Jesus' promise, we may surmise that the sooner we locate the sheep, the sooner He will come again. Matthew 28:19–20 makes sure our calling *and* our Companion. So, it is a given that we must preach, teach, and gather.

But, I am suggesting an even more drastic tactic. In fact, this is the one place that America is doing pretty well, today. I would say that America even deserves a global award in this area. And, that is in the arena of compassion, charity, and good deeds. I know we don't see it on the cable news, or hear of it often, but kindness and unselfish giving is alive and well in the U.S.A.

Every time a teacher goes the extra mile to stimulate greatness in a student, or a community places collection jars at the local gas station market to raise funds for a terminally ill child, or a person of substance gives of their time and money to build schools, or provide medicines, or dig water wells, or the neighbors of a widow cut her grass or do her shopping, or families gather to bless or pray for a loved one, or quick-thinking hero jumps into icy water to retrieve an accident victim, or a focused public servant enters a dangerous area to look for the lost, or someone's ego moves out of the way on the highway or in a grocery store line, acts of mercy and compassion are present.

Two teenagers cooked up an idea to provide discarded cell phones to our troops in Iraq so they can call home. A young boy started a drive to donate blankets to street people. A restaurant owner purchases and prepares Thanksgiving dinner, yearly, to the needy. Food drives pepper (no pun intended) American Saturday mornings. Abused animals are taken to sanctuaries for rehabilitation from the jaws of puppy mills, dog fight yards, and flooded out neighborhoods. Whole families were "adopted" by other families, often miles away, after Hurricane Katrina and brought to live with them until they were back on their feet. We send food, and supplies, and money, and missionaries to Africa, Indonesia, China, India, Myanmar, Afghanistan, Cambodia, South Korea, Ukraine, and the list goes on and on. Everywhere human beings suffer or are in need, Americas can be found reaching out as far as governments will allow. Yes, America has a heart.

Still, as God's elect children, the Christians must fulfill this calling with the understanding that we are representatives and not just fellow sojourners. I do not desire to desecrate the heroic deeds of kindness and compassion aforementioned. In fact, I stand in awe of them. My comment is for those who know, with true assurance, from whence every good thing cometh. If you do not like that concept, and really believe that humankind performs random acts of kindness as an out-cropping of their innate goodness, this note is not for you.

God has called his people to be salt and light. He has called us to conform to the image of His Son. We are to be Jesus to the world because we know that Jesus is alive and seated on the right hand of the Father in the Heavenly throne room. You know what I mean. WWJD is cute. But, try replacing the last word *Do* with the word *Deserve*, and then you have a Christian heart. We perform good works *because* we are His, new heart and all.

I like to reflect on the words of the plaque positioned beneath the Statue of Liberty in the New York City harbor. The inscription comes from a poem written by Emma Lazarus in 1883. She was Jewish by descent and became deeply moved by the plight of Jewish immigrants to America who had lost everything, including their homeland.

It is tender for me because my own grandmother came to these shores, barely fourteen years old, alone and displaced. Grandma worked in a tuna canning factory earning two cents for each can sealed. She bore this burden until enough money had been raised to bring the rest of her family to freedom, just months before Hitler's armies occupied their hometown. And, I think my life is unbearable when the air conditioning does not work.

The history of this country is awe-inspiring and humbling. We cannot allow its demise. As Emma Lazarus wrote:

> "Give me your tired, your poor, your huddled masses
> yearning to breathe free, the wretched refuse
> of your teeming shore. Send these the homeless,
> tempest-tost to me. I lift my lamp beside the golden door."

I like to fancy that inscription on the doors of Heaven.

Sisters, our lamp is out of oil. We did not plan well. There is still time to prepare for the Bridegroom. So, let the silly ones revel on. Get to work shining the light in all the dark corners, stroke the fevered brow of the suffering, demand righteousness and justice, force obedience if you have to, and be about your Father's business. Time is short.

And, last but most certainly not least, pray without ceasing.

> "Rejoice always, pray without ceasing, in everything give
> thanks; for this is the will of God in Christ Jesus for you."
>
> 1 Thess. 5:16–18

> *"The effective, fervent prayer of a righteous man avails much."*
>
> JAMES 5:16B

> *"—but we will give ourselves continually to prayer and to the ministry of the word."*
>
> ACTS 6:4

> *"Let love be without hypocrisy. Abhor what is evil. Cling to what is good. Be kindly affectionate to one another with brotherly love, in honor giving preference to one another; not lagging in diligence, fervent in spirit, serving the Lord; rejoicing in hope, patient in tribulation, **continuing steadfastly in prayer**; distributing to the needs of the saints, given to hospitality."*
>
> ROMANS 12:9–12

I should just stop there. In fact, the entire chapter is summed up in that one reference from Romans, chapter 12. God will always prove Himself to be a better writer than I.

However, I am not insensitive to the fact that persistent reminders are the best way to force the internalization of a truth. I began this book entreating Christian women to rise up and champion the battle. I wish the battle was a new one that could be won once for all. It is not. It must be fought every day and every minute.

> *"Finally, my brethren, be strong in the Lord and in the power of His might. Put on the whole armor of God, that you may be able to stand against the wiles of the devil. For we do not wrestle against flesh or blood, but against principalities, against powers, against the rulers of the darkness of this age, against spiritual hosts of wickedness in the heavenly places. Therefore take up the whole armor of God, that you may be able to withstand in the evil day, and having done all, to stand."*
>
> EPHESIANS 6:10–13

Lest my readers who fancy themselves to be more rational than spiritual begin to feel pounded by the scripture, consider these words of the poet J. G. Holland, penned just following the horrors of our country's Civil War.

> "God Give Us Men!"
> God give us men! A time like this demands
> Strong minds, great hearts, true faith and ready hands;
> Men whom the lust of office does not kill;
> Men whom the spoils of office cannot buy;
> Men who possess opinions and a will;
> Men who have honor; men who will not lie;
> Men who can stand before a demagogue
> And damn his treacherous flatteries without winking!
> Tall men, sun-crowned, who live above the fog
> In public duty, and in private thinking;
> For while the rabble, with their thumb-worn creeds;
> Their large professions and their little deeds,
> Mingle in selfish strife, lo! Freedom weeps,
> Wrong rules the land and waiting Justice sleeps.
>
> JOSIAH GILBERT HOLLAND

Deborah saw to it that Barak was that man. Take off your apron. We have work to do. By the way, for whom are you voting?

Epilogue

Some Assembly Required

> *"But each one is tempted when he is drawn away by his own desires and enticed. Then, when desire has conceived, it gives birth to sin; and sin, when it is full-grown, brings forth death. Do not be deceived, my beloved brethren. Every good gift and every perfect gift is from above, and comes down from the Father of lights, with whom there is no variation or shadow of turning. Of His own will He brought us forth by the word of truth, that we might be a kind of firstfruits of His creatures."*
>
> JAMES 1:14–18

IN THE CLASSIC PLAY "Our Town" by Thornton Wilder, the matter-of-fact attitude of the stage manager, who is also the narrator, makes many references to the nature of things. As I come to my closing remarks, I am reminded of one of his quixotic lines, which appears to be almost an afterthought intended for segue. He observes: "Wind's comin' up, seems like." I know that line did not make the top ten list of study guide quotes. Nevertheless, that observation is keenly important to life in a small farming community and applies in an illustrative way to my final note, here. You see, wind portends something. Often, a sudden movement of air velocity means that a deadly storm is on its windy way. It tells us to take cover or to strengthen the protective barriers. And, if there are others for whom we are responsible, the gathering storm may demand that we battle the elements in order to collect our figurative chicks and bring them to safety.

So that you do not conclude that I have gone completely mad, allow me to provide analysis. I began this book by reflecting on the state of our nation and the world. By very nature of my chosen heroine, the presupposed foundational issue is the relevance of the Biblical sin cycle to the trauma of the day. If you had not been experiencing some discomfort or even rage relative to our national circumstance, this book would not have appealed to you nor have even been purchased by you. So, we can agree that America, and more specifically God's people, have a problem. I think, that at this point in our discussion, it is clear that the problem, to all who reason, is drastic. In chapter twelve, we took all of the data, added up the columns, and deduced that "*We the people*" are doing evil in the sight of a Holy God.

Usually, at this point in any social gathering, the women pick up the evacuated casserole dishes, the children begin whining for permission to play just one more minute, and the men commence the perfunctory head shake, often commenting about the lack of power we all have to change the course of our imminent destruction. In other words, back to business as usual and off to our pillows we go. As you know, I will not stand for that sort of pusillanimous copping out. It is roll up the sleeves time and down on your knees time. In other words, pay close attention to the formulation of the next play. You will be required to perform.

If the last chapter could be considered a "wish list", this chapter must be considered a "to do" list. The oft forgotten responsibility of those who have become aware of a serious situation is the obligatory necessity to act. Since I have now postulated that our dilemma must be understood by the juxtaposition of all of its components into a salient action plan, it is mandatory to present the plan. You see, I could scatter all of the parts of a great mountain bike across the floor in my study and then show all of my friends my bike. But, you know well that a bike only achieves bike-ness when it can be ridden. And so, we see the challenges before us. Now, what do we do with this mess?

When Barak hesitated in the execution of God's commands, Deborah launched a presumptive strike. When Jonah headed for the wrong hill, the fish regurgitated him back on track. When Sisera demanded sanctuary in the tent of Jael, she courageously took his life. When the soldiers sought to capture the disciples, Rahab defied Roman authority and conspired to protect. In the land of promise, when oppression became unbearable, the people cried out for deliverance. During the inter-testamental era, the Maccabees plotted and carried out acts of civil disobedience against

Roman tyranny. Paul, John, the Baptist, both James', Peter, and later Polycarp, and others were severally or individually imprisoned, tortured, stoned, beaten, burned, beheaded, hung, and savaged without giving up one tenet of the truth. I could go on and on. You get the point.

If you are still looking for some concrete direction, try these:

> "Therefore whoever hears these stories of Mine, and does them, I will liken him to a wise man who built his house on a rock: and the rain descended, the floods came, and the winds blew and beat on that house; and, it did not fall, for it was founded on the rock. But, everyone who hears these sayings of Mine, and does not do them, will be like a foolish man who built his house on the sand: and the rain descended, the floods came, and the winds blew and beat on that house; and it fell. And, great was its fall."
>
> MATTHEW 7:24–27

> "You know that the rulers of the Gentiles lord it over them, and those who are great exercise authority over them. Yet, it shall not be so among you; but, whoever desires to become great among you, let him be your servant. And whoever desires to be first among you, let him be your slave—just as the Son of Man did not come to be served, but to serve, and to give His life a ransom for many."
>
> MATTHEW 20:25B–28

> "Now I rejoice, not that you were made sorry, but that your sorrow led to repentance. For you were made sorry in a godly manner, that you might suffer loss from us in nothing. For godly sorrow produces repentance, leading to salvation, not to be regretted; but the sorrow of the world produces death."
>
> 2 CORINTHIANS 7:9–10

> "When leaders lead in Israel,
> When the people willingly offer themselves,
> Bless the Lord."
>
> JUDGES 5:2 (SONG OF DEBORAH)

> *"Thus let all your enemies perish, O Lord!*
> *But let those who love Him be like the sun*
> *When it comes out in full strength.*
> *So the land had rest for forty years."*
>
> Judges 5:31 (Song of Deborah)

> *"For behold, the day is coming. Burning like an oven, and all the proud, yes, all who do wickedly will be stubble. And the day which is coming shall burn them up. Says the Lord of hosts, that will leave them neither root nor branch. But to you who fear my Name the Son of Righteousness shall arise with healing in His wings; and you shall go out and grow fat like stall-fed calves. You shall trample the wicked. For they shall be ashes under the soles of your feet on the day that I do this, says the Lord of hosts."*
> *"And He will turn the hearts of the fathers to the children, and the hearts of the children to their fathers..."*
>
> Malachi 4:1–3, 6a

> *"I charge you therefore before God and the Lord Jesus Christ, who will judge the living and the dead at His appearing and His kingdom. Preach the word! Be ready in season and out of season. Convince, rebuke, exhort, with all the long- suffering and teaching. For the time will come when they will not endure sound doctrine, but according to their own desires because they have itching ears, they will heap up for them-selves teachers, and they will turn their ears away from the truth, and be turned aside to fables. But you be watchful in all things endure afflictions, do the work of an evangelist, fulfill your ministry."*
>
> 2 Timothy 4:1–5

And so, my friends, vote, caucus, run for office, petition, sign petitions, lobby, tithe, support godly candidates, speak out at council meetings, write your congressmen, submit letters to the editor of your local paper, study and be highly educated in the processes of freedom, train your children to love the Lord and our country, hold public servants accountable, rebuke a weaker brother (or sister), go to the gate of the city until you are heard, stand in the gap, fight for the unborn, picket the wicked, call out to God for wisdom and deliverance, and *pray, pray, pray*.

For the sake of our country, our children, and our moral ethic, I pray for deliverance. I cry out to the Lord for mercy. This is altogether our darkest and our finest hour. Let us meet it with dignity and integrity. To that end, I offer this final warning. "Wind's comin' up seems like."

Salvation Invitation

IT IS NOT OFTEN that a book of such political persuasion includes within it an invitation of eternal importance. This one does. I can think of no greater solution to the issues of the day than a worldwide realization of our need for a Savior.

If you stand today as a saved Christian, I humbly extend my gratitude for your reading of this book and pray that it has blessed you as you step out in faith to heal our land. If, however, you have not accepted Jesus Christ as your Lord and Savior, I implore you to do so, now. The world is, at best, a risky business with few certain promises and outcomes. The God who created us offers the only certainty upon which we can depend. Please, do not miss this gift.

For those whose heart has been touched by these simple words, please pray this prayer: "Dear Lord, I come to you a sinner, frustrated and empty pleading to be filled with your peace and comfort. These are troubled times when fear and uncertainty grip our hearts. I ask for Your forgiveness and mercy to save me today according to Your certain promise. Please come into my heart and guide and guard the rest of my days. I set myself before you, a willing sacrifice, and petition for the strength and courage to follow your Will. Thank-you, Lord, for the sacrifice made on the cross in my behalf, and for the resurrection on the third day that made clear my way home to You. Amen."

Or, just use your own words. God probably likes you better, anyway. Just kidding.

www.ingramcontent.com/pod-product-compliance
Lightning Source LLC
Chambersburg PA
CBHW050834160426
43192CB00010B/2027